◆ FriesenPress

One Printers Way
Altona, MB R0G 0B0
Canada

www.friesenpress.com

ISBN
978-1-03-917656-0 (Hardcover)
978-1-03-917655-3 (Paperback)
978-1-03-917657-7 (eBook)

1. BODY, MIND & SPIRIT, MINDFULNESS & MEDITATION

Distributed to the trade by The Ingram Book Company

Thelma Wheatley

To Thelma!   age 82 (almost)

You are very kindful!

Bhante Saranapala

Nov. 15, 2023

Are You Kindful?

How your practice of
kindfulness can build a
happy and peaceful nation

BHANTE SARANAPALA
The Urban Buddhist Monk

Table of Contents

Foreword

"In the garden of life, we all do shine,
With love and light, with sacred Divine.
Look up to the stars and you will see they are all aligned.
As it is a new era, a new time, a new conscious state of mind."

— MITCH ABRAMS

Welcome friends!

My name is Mitch Abrams. I am a Canadian radiologist, teacher, and certified Ambassador of Compassion. I have dedicated my life to compassion: to understanding compassion, to teaching tools of compassion, and to serving, supporting, and inspiring the integration of compassion—both in health care and the everyday lives of others. I have embarked on a mission to forge new frontiers of compassion to both benefit my fellow global citizens and humanity as a whole.

It was only recently that I received my official ambassadorship from Stanford's School of Medicine's Center of Compassion and Altruism Research and Education (CCARE). After extensively studying the science of compassion and working with other compassion pioneers around the world, I have been bestowed the great responsibility and honour to provide a foreword for Dr. Bhante Saranapala's new book.

Dr. Bhante Saranapala—whom many of you know as the Urban Buddhist Monk—has been spreading the message and work of compassion for years. Through his teachings and guided meditations—both at the Buddhist temple and abroad—Dr. Bhante has been a prominent and true champion of compassion the world over. Through his one-on-one support sessions and through his many community projects, he is helping provide life's necessities to those in need.

I was blessed to meet Bhante almost eight years ago, after I returned from India where I was exploring the ancient wisdom of the Vedic traditions of healing. I still remember Bhante's gentle laughter and beaming smile as I approached him at his temple all those years ago. I was elated to meet Bhante as I had recently begun getting serendipitous messages that I was to meet a wise Buddhist practitioner as part of my ongoing exploration. I still remember Bhante's short and simple reply to my diatribe. I excitedly tried to express to Bhante how I felt, that there were no coincidences in life, that events we believe to be serendipitous could be understood and explained through a quantum reality, and that my heart was deeply impassioned with learning more of the ancient ways of mindfulness and whole person healing. I explained that there had to be a reason we were being introduced at this particular moment, and I knew I was exactly where I was meant to be, drinking chai and conversing with a smiling Buddhist monk. Despite my enthusiasm, Bhante quietly responded with a simple and concise "of course" and shared a laugh that can only be described as infectious. I knew at that very moment that Dr. Bhante Saranapala and I would become lifelong friends and colleagues in the field of compassion.

For years following our meeting, Bhante and I worked on many projects together as we continued to spread awareness about the power of kindness and compassion. I could feel Bhante's appreciation for my sense of purpose and for our mutually aligned mission in helping people access their true potential, a potential realized through the cultivation of compassion for oneself. I immediately began to recognize how effective Dr. Bhante was at helping people work through their mental, emotional, and even physical pain; how skilled he was at guiding people to find a safe place to land their hurting hearts; and how intuitively he provided a roadmap to peace for people's state of mind. As a medical physician, I was honoured to begin spreading compassion alongside Bhante. I recognized his numerous powerfully effective gifts: his ability to help people rewire their brains in just the right way and find inner peace and tranquility through simple mental exercises, which ultimately resulted in the rewiring of their neural circuitry.

I have been honoured to be a presenter at many of Bhante's Making Canada a Mindful and Kind Nation symposiums. Bhante has gathered the nation's experts on the science of compassion to share and learn together. At these symposiums, I had many opportunities to share the emerging science of compassion.

I see Bhante as a practitioner of health, with a subspecialty in the field of non-invasive neurosurgery. Bhante's teachings of ancient mindful techniques and the exploration into the nature of our humanity help people find their inherent strength and their capacity to meet life's challenges. Bhante's teachings literally help people rewire their neutral circuitry—a form of non-invasive brain surgery.

In this age of ever-increasing stress, our collective well-being is being impacted. This impact is so severe that for the first time since 1900, life expectancy decreased in relation to the previous generation. We are heading in the wrong direction. This is why Dr. Bhante's work is so critical.

In 2016 Bhante started a movement: Canada, A Mindful and Kind Nation. His work is impressive and promotes teachings that help people become kind and compassionate to themselves and others. What we know from the science of compassion is that compassion is contagious. In fact, when we learn to be compassionate to ourselves, not only do we begin to address and resolve our own personal mental health challenges, but we find a greater capacity to be compassionate to others.

As a Certified Compassionate Ambassador, I want to explain to you exactly how compassion affects your physiology and the physiology of those around you. Yes, acts of compassion not only affect your physiology, but the physiology of others. Research clearly shows that the more we understand ourselves and how our amazing biological technology functions, the more likely we are to put our understanding into practice—in this case, the practice of compassion.

The science of compassion is truly fascinating. It reveals the secrets of not only our true human nature, but also our interconnectedness. There is a term in medical literature called coherence. Coherence describes a state when sub-systems are synchronized with each other, creating a powerful synergy. This synergy results in an optimal state of function in which the sum is greater than its parts. For instance, if musicians of a symphony are not synchronized, the resulting effect is incoherent noise. When the musicians are synchronized, as when the conductor brings each individual musician into appropriate timing with another, what results is a beautifully coherent piece of music. It turns out the human body is no different. We can cultivate a state of coherence, which has significant implications for our mental, physical, emotional, and spiritual well-being. Compassion is inherently connected to this state of coherence.

Before explaining this dynamic relationship between compassion and coherence, let me explain some interesting facts about your heart.

Most cultures understand compassion as a function of, or an expression of, our heart. Interestingly, modern science is proving this age-old view. A relatively new field of research, called neurocardiology, focuses on the heart-brain and its relationship to the brain in our heads. The heart-brain is a small collection of brain cells—the same brain cells that support proteins and neurochemicals as the big brain in your head—but this heart-brain is actually located in your heart. Dr. Armour, in 1991, published a paper describing this little brain in our hearts.

This little brain demonstrates the same capabilities as the brain in our head. It learns from, and reacts to, our environment, both internal and external. It has memory, both short term and long term. It is intelligent and functions independent of the big brain. In fact, despite its smaller size, the heart-brain has a significant impact on the functionality of the brain.

One of the many functions of the heart-brain is to convert your emotional states into heart rhythms. How intriguing it is that your mental state is encoded in the rhythms of your heart. Specifically, the interbeat interval—the time between each beat—which varies slightly from beat to beat and is known as heart rate variability (HRV). When experiencing anger, fear, anxiety, or any such negative emotion, your HRV becomes very irregular. This irregular HRV is called incoherent. When feeling appreciation, love, compassion, or any other positive emotion, your HRV becomes very regular and rhythmic and is referred to as coherent. The coherence or incoherence of your heart rate variability has significant effects on your mental health, cognitive capacity, and overall health and well-being.

This brings us back to the symphony and the relationship between compassion and coherence. It turns out that our heart functions like the conductor of a symphony, coordinating all our organ systems like musicians. By coordinating each musician and getting each organ system to synchronize, our entire energetic system begins to synchronize, establishing an optimal energetic state. Research shows that this state of coherence boosts our inherent capacity to heal ourselves and thrive. It also optimizes our biological systems and modulates the expression of our genes. When the heart is incoherent, as a result of stress or anxiety, the irregular heart rhythms fail to synchronize our organ systems and result in an inefficient energetic state. This inefficient incoherent state drains our energy—our life force— contributes greatly to illness and disease, and inhibits our capacity to thrive. Additionally, our heart rhythms, be they coherent or incoherent, greatly affect our mental health and our ability to perform.

The rhythms from the heart are sent up to the brain, specifically, to the thalamus. The thalamus is like a relay station, relaying the information to the more evolved parts of our brain that affect our cognitive capacities. In a state of coherence, the regular rhythmic signals from the heart synchronize with the brain, which in turn cause the brainwaves to synchronize with the heart rhythms and create an optimal state of consciousness. It is in this state that we perform at our best, our memory is optimized, we are attuned to the present, and we feel we are in the flow of life with total ease and grace. The converse however, is when we are incoherent. In a state of incoherence, the irregular signals are relayed to the brain, and because the signals are incoherent, synchronization does not take place. The result is an inhibited state, an inefficient state that drains our energy and prevents optimal performance. The noisy signal from the heart shorts the brain, preventing it from functioning optimally.

Recall a time of great stress in your life, a time when you had to perform but struggled. Perhaps this occurred during an exam, a speech, a presentation, or even a sporting event. Have you ever experienced a moment when you were so anxious that you could not recall the simplest of facts for your exam? Two plus two became challenging. You fumbled the layup you'd practised a million times, or your mind went blank when reciting the speech you'd rehearsed flawlessly. You were in a state of incoherence.

Alternately, when feeling good, excited, or in the flow of life, your coherent heart rhythm causes your brain to be facilitated and optimized. The answers become intuitive and that layup is effortless. This optimal state of being is greatly attributed to your state of coherence, which is the result of your emotional state.

Compassion and coherence go hand in hand. When you feel compassion, for either yourself or others, your heart-brain translates the energy you are experiencing into a coherent heart rhythm. Simply put, compassion cultivates coherence. Compassion synchronizes your biological rhythms and causes your entire physiology to vibrate at a higher frequency, which ultimately unlocks your true potential to heal, thrive, and perform. For the avid science lovers among you, the optimal coherence frequency that your heart and entire energetic system vibrates at is noted to be 0.1 Hz, which happens to be the same frequency as the first magnetic field line of our planet Earth. Perhaps you are starting to see the big picture now . . .

Now this is where things get super interesting. Not only does compassion cultivate a state of coherence that optimizes your mental, physical, and emotional health, but it also induces others around you to become coherent. YES!! Your compassion, your love for self, and your love for others can actually pull other people's hearts into a coherent rhythm. This, in turn, affects how they think, act, and respond to themselves and others. Your self-care and emotional state have a direct impact on the people around you.

As Einstein famously said, everything is energy. You are an energetic being, and the emotions you experience are energies that are not contained within yourself. Your energy affects your environment and those around you. Your energy directly affects the energy of your friends, your family, your colleagues, and your communities—locally and globally.

To further illustrate this point, I will refer you to a research project published in a peer reviewed journal article: "Effects of Group Practice of the Transcendental Meditation Program on Preventing Violent Crime in Washington, DC: Results of the National Demonstration Project, June–July 1993," conducted by Dr. J. Hagelin et al. The hypothesis was that a large group of individuals would come together in Washington, DC, for two months and practise a specific mental exercise that cultivated compassion. This would, in turn, create coherence, and collectively, this coherent field of energy would reduce the local crime rate. In fact, the authors calculated that for the community size of Washington, in order to drop their crime rate by 20 percent, they required four thousand participants to join the study and help cultivate this energetic coherence. The police chief at the time thought they were crazy and colourfully shared his opinion.

After more than three years of intense peer review (which is an unprecedented amount of time to review the validity of the research design), the results were published in a mainstream peer reviewed journal. The crime rate had indeed decreased by 23 percent by the end of the two months, with approximately four thousand participants focusing on compassion for self and others. What is also interesting to note, is that the crime rate rebounded to baseline values following the study, as people went back to where they came from.

This phenomenon has been replicated and verified by multiple subsequent research studies and is becoming better understood. Coherence plays a key role in the science of connectedness and is a key tenet for the co-creation of healthy, thriving, compassionate communities.

So, as you can see, Dr. Bhante Saranapala's work with compassion is needed now more than ever. His work not only helps

Dalai Lama?

people handle life's challenges, but it also helps spread compassion around the world, which can be felt and seen on many levels. From providing humanitarian aid to countries and communities in need to sending love and compassion into a collective field of compassion that we are all connected to, Dr. Bhante Saranapala is changing our landscape of love in measurable ways.

The study of coherence, the heart-brain connection, and the interconnectedness of all of humanity is remarkably empowering. We now understand the link between self-care and social activism. The world changes as we change how we feel about ourselves. People who hurt others are themselves hurting. Joan Compassion heals the emotional wounds we all bear, and through compassionate self-exploration, you are subconsciously helping others around you. We are entering an exciting new chapter in health care that is as much local as it is global in scope. We should all feel blessed for people like Bhante, who are dedicated to the service of others, who are spreading the art and science of self-care, and who are creating opportunities to spread compassion and much needed assistance to those in need.

As part of my obligation as a Certified Ambassador of Compassion with Stanford's CCARE, I created a framework for a new sustainable funding model called RADDical A.R.T. This initiative leverages the power of art to educate, heal, and inspire communities. It is a sustainable "funding mechanism," which transforms the sharing of knowledge about coherence and compassion into tangible value, and leverages the power of art to support mental health and resilience programming for communities in need.

In brief, I collaborate with a talented pool of artists who have graduated from the RADDical A.R.T. Residency Program. This program is based on my accredited curriculum for physicians and health-care providers. The artists are invited to join me for all my educational programs and keynotes, and for many amazing conversations with compassion champions. They work in the background to produce a piece of live art during the program (and, in some cases, create collaborative pieces as they incorporate contributions from participants). The artists are able to capture these meaningful moments of sharing and learning together. These are precious moments of connection that result from the transfer of knowledge and the birth of a new expanded perspective of our common humanity. In this way, the certified artists become change makers and "practitioners of health." The pieces become part of our RADDical A.R.T. Collection and are sold or sponsored, generating fundraising to support the delivery of more programs.

I warmly invite you all to use the link below to tune into a RADDical A.R.T. event with Dr. Bhante Saranapala as we discuss his new book and the amazing compassionate work that is spreading around the world. https://nexgenhealth.solutions/BhanteS

I wish you all a coherent heart and brain as you continue down the road of compassion with Bhante.

May we all be well. May we all be happy. May we all find peace and be free.

From my heart to yours,

Dr. Mitch Abrams, MD, FRCPC
Certified Ambassador of Compassion, Stanford, CCARE

Part One

The Vision Unfolded

CHAPTER 1

A Vision for a Kindful Nation

"Gratitude makes sense of our past, brings peace for today, and creates a vision for tomorrow."

— MELODY BEATTIE

Sowing the Seeds

Although my motivation for writing this book fell upon me several years ago, the vision itself was very much inspired by my childhood experiences and by my upbringing. Throughout my life, kindfulness—the art of combining both kindness and mindfulness—is something I have been fortunate enough to experience, practise, and share with the people who come to meet me. Being a monk who meets a diverse array of people, I have seen how the concept of a kindful world ignites a light in their eyes. People who experience this kindness and mindfulness are better able to manage the difficulties they face in the world.

After years of contemplating and recognizing how passing along the gift of kindfulness instills hope in others, I have decided to work toward creating a mindful and kind world starting with Canada, the country that has given me so much. I then want to follow that by spreading the message out, gradually, to all countries.

This important mission is how the charitable initiative, Canada: A Mindful and Kind Nation was born in 2016. It is my calling to spread the message of kindfulness to the globe. I told a long-time friend Michael Weldon and a long-time meditation student Jenny Kim of my goal. They agreed that bringing kindfulness to the masses needed to become reality.

This calling would not have arisen without a lifetime of momentum. Just as adding drops of water to a jar can slowly fill it over time, so too was my inspiration the product of decades of receiving kindfulness, starting in my childhood with the kindness of my grandfather, the memory of which still stands out to this day.

* * *

I was born in 1972 and grew up in a small village in Bangladesh. It certainly had its benefits, not the least of which was being able to gather with the children of the village and play. My grandfather, a well-respected citizen of the village, would watch with a warm smile as we frolicked about. Like a shepherd rounding up his flock, he would then beckon for us to come, bringing us all within earshot with a slight grin pulling at the corners of his mouth. When he managed to settle us down, he would play a little game.

My grandfather would begin reciting various sayings and telling us to repeat after him.

"We are going to be engineers . . . we are going to be presidents . . . we are going to be doctors!" he would say with warmth and conviction, only for dozens of little voices to squeak out the same. As he proclaimed each statement, his momentum and energy grew to a raucous and thundering roar.

"We are going to be intelligent . . . we are going to be great minds and hearts . . . we are going to be the most loving and caring people in the world!" he would bellow with a joyous smile, with us eagerly doing the same.

My grandfather believed strongly in education and saw a future for us that was brighter than the world he had grown up in. He wisely observed that this bright future was based on the success and well-being of not just the generations of the past, but also of those present here and now, as well as the generations to come. Perhaps most importantly, his heart was filled with love and kindness for all the children of the village.

In later years, I would tag along with my grandfather on rickshaw rides. Though he never alluded to it or spun tales of gossip regarding the affairs of others, his watchful eye observed when families in the village were struggling. On a typical ride, he would spontaneously veer off the road, pull into the rickshaw park of a home, and hop out to drop off a package filled with fresh fruits and vegetables. Though this made little sense to me as a child, in later years I was able to reflect on the manner in which my grandfather's generosity silently and humbly influenced the village, ensuring that others were always loved and supported.

As I grew older, and with the passing of both time and my grandfather, I came to observe these same traits of kindfulness in his daughter, my mother. As his eldest child, she was always the leader of the pack. Even when in her elderly and sick state, she would attempt to find ways of helping the village. In 2015, when my mother passed away, I flew from Canada to be present for her funeral in Bangladesh. Two days after the funeral, on my walk down the main road of the village, I was stopped in the street by a Muslim man.

"Excuse me!" he called out. "Are you the son of the lady who just passed away?" he asked quizzically.

"Yes, I am," I responded.

"Your mother was so generous. Anytime you sent her vitamins or snacks, she would share them with us!" He burst into tears, exclaiming, "She was such a kind person! What a loss to all of us!"

Occasions like this remind me that the power of generosity transcends religious differences.

* * *

I became a novice monk in 1984, and in the years to come, I witnessed bountiful kindness from my great monastic teachers. I saw my senior monastic principal establish many shelters out of love and compassion for the people in the village. Impoverished and struggling families, who were unable to afford to send their kids to school or have hot meals on the table, would be provided with a roof over their head and a full stomach. Many of the youth who passed through those shelters went on to attain higher education and become inspiring spiritual leaders.

Later in 1984, when I moved to Sri Lanka and was taken under the tutelage of another monastic teacher, I was granted the privilege of taking part in charitable school programs. My monastic teacher organized one such charitable initiative whereby children and parents from wealthier schools were encouraged to donate whatever they could—without any expectations— if they were able to and out of the generosity of their heart. In some cases, the donations were just a single pencil, but in others, hundreds of dollars worth of backpacks, notebooks, and non-perishable food items were given. When the items were donated, the other monks and I would drive around to the participating schools, hop out, and load up the trucks. Once the trucks were fully loaded, we would drive to the rural schools where resources were lacking, drop off these donations, unload the trucks, and pack the items away. We would often do this in the hot sun, dripping in sweat, but with smiles on our faces. Why smiles, you ask? Because it was great fun! There was an inherent sense of joy in knowing we were directly assisting those in need, which made the effort feel worthwhile.

Establishing New Roots

When I came to Canada in 1995, thanks to the kindness of my Sri Lankan teacher, the Most Venerable Muditha Nayaka Mahathera, I settled at the West End Buddhist Temple and Meditation Centre in Mississauga, Ontario. I was greeted by the familiar friend I had come to know: kindness. This time, kindness came in the form of the Chief Abbot of the temple, the Most Venerable Dhammawasa Nayaka Mahathera. He was constantly extending a helping hand to people in need. When the temple was first established, he would take in refugees and newcomers who were unable to make ends meet. He would welcome anyone into the temple, providing sweet treats and snacks, which to this day are overshadowed only by his warm and loving smile. His assistance would go beyond simple niceties and politeness. He would actively help people find work, get an education, and obtain the essentials. He was a consistent source of support as these families attempted to get on their feet.

Soon after my arrival in Canada, I took over the responsibility of teaching the basics of meditation at the temple's Wednesday night meditation classes where a "crowd" of about ten lay practitioners would be considered a feat. It seldom occurred. Nevertheless, I recognized the increased joy and peace that arose in those who would show up, week after week, to simply sit quietly in a supportive environment and learn to meditate. The words spoken were not always remembered, but the atmosphere of kindness, care, and unconditional acceptance made all the difference. This happiness and joy were the product of the same kindness I had experienced throughout my life, manifesting itself in a new form. It is the kindness that says, "You're OK here, just as you are, no matter your race, religion, gender, sexual orientation, social status, physical (dis)abilities, or any other discernible marker. All are welcome."

As I continued to teach people how to be kind and mindful, I noticed a trend. Each week, there would be a few new faces. Occasionally, these new additions would timidly approach me with a friend after the meditation class, and one of the pair would blurt out "Bhante, I've been coming to your class for months now, and I was finally able to drag my friend out! I wanted to introduce you to them!" Soon, I started to notice an increase in the number of meditation cushions needed each week to account for this growing interest.

I can't quite say when it happened, but one Wednesday evening, I walked into the meditation class and noticed that every single meditation cushion was occupied. The walls were lined with people from the sides to the back of the meditation hall.

Over the course of almost three decades, I've taught meditation to Buddhists, Christians, Muslims, Jews, atheists, and agnostics alike. Thanks to my Canadian brother, Troy MacLean, I've worked directly with, and influenced, educators, emergency responders, political leaders, and activists. I've taught the basics of meditation to non-governmental organizations, corporations, and entrepreneurs. Since 2016, I have been teaching members of the Peel and Toronto police how to meditate.

The privilege of meeting all these wonderful Canadians and the opportunity to teach and share stories with them are together a reflection of the beautiful opportunities Canada provides and the natural capacity for kindness so strongly present in the spirit of the country. Throughout these interactions, I've seen the incredible tendency toward kindness average citizens embody, the ability of diverse peoples to rise to the occasion and act in a way that is fair, compassionate, honest, and empowering.

Recently, a pair of sisters, ages three and five, came for a visit with their parents. These sisters were familiar faces at a Sunday school I run for children, but whom I had not seen in quite some time due to COVID restrictions. After being away for quite some time, they began begging their parents to return when the restrictions lifted. I learned that they had missed the smiles and sweet treats the other monks and I had become known for at the temple. The sugar may have been the primary motivating factor, but the warmth and joy kept them hooked. It is this same warmth and joy that the people of this country have shown us and which we now have the privilege of returning through these small acts of generosity.

The Motivation of Compassion

Being generously welcomed to this country and given the opportunity to flourish through the donations of lay devotees and supporters, I now feel compelled to give something back. Being a simple Buddhist monk living with few personal belongings and surviving from donations and one simple meal per day, I cannot offer anything material. However, I believe that what I can give holds great value. The gift I offer is the opportunity to take your life into your own hands and gain the ability to take control of your happiness.

After decades of living in Canada, of teaching meditation to people from all walks of life, and of hearing of the variety of lived experiences, the common thread I have seen is that people struggle. This struggle occurs no matter who you are, regardless of political affiliations, religious or cultural backgrounds, poverty or wealth, fame, or disrepute. It is the struggle common to all human beings, and it manifests itself as discontent, dissatisfaction, unhappiness, suffering, anguish, or simply a general feeling of want, lack, or missing something that would make you whole. It is the struggle for meaning in our daily lived experiences. If we learn how to work with this inner struggle, we can live a life of true freedom. However, if we never aspire to resolve this tension, we become shackled like prisoners, wandering about searching for a balm to soothe the pain, never knowing the feeling of true happiness.

What I am going to share in the coming pages is applicable to anyone. The wisdom that follows is not from a place of blind faith or dogmatic ritualism. Rather, it is from my having seen and heard the experiences of thousands of people and their testimonies on the impact the practice of kindfulness has had on their happiness. This book is my attempt to impart knowledge, and my genuine attempt to elevate everyone's state of happiness.

Most importantly, these teachings do not belong to any particular history, culture, religion, or nationality. What follows is my call to action, a reminder that we, as human beings, are all capable of living up to a higher ideal and that we all have our own individual role to play in this regard. The call is simply this one word: kindfulness.

We are all the recipients of boundless kindness. It is now time to act. Though some of the lessons my grandfather and teachers passed on may have long faded from my memory, the most important one remains. Kindfulness is living life in a way that embodies kindness. Just as countless others have passed this on to us, there is a need, now more than ever, to pass this message on to future generations.

If you've picked up this book, you are ready to answer this call.

Knowing Where We Stand

Before providing you with my vision for a kindful nation, I feel it would be helpful to take an inventory of where we stand, collectively, as a nation. Much like a sculptor seeking to replicate a fine Constantin Brancusi or a hockey coach writing a playbook for the upcoming playoff series, it helps to know the playing field and what raw materials you are working with.

The seed of kindness is indeed present in our values, ethics, and collective conduct. American comedians often joke that Canadians are kind to a fault, and indeed, observing the number of "sorrys," "please," and "thank-yous" we repeat in daily interactions with strangers can seem comical at times. This tendency toward cohesion and a kindful nature is not just an act or social trend, but is rooted in what we inherently associate with Canadian values. On the global stage, Canada's image is received as a very positive, kind, and peaceful nation. When I travel to deliver talks, people often tell me how kind and friendly Canadians are and how nice it must be that I have the opportunity to live in Canada. Many of my disciples often confide in me that when they travel and inform others that they are from Canada, people immediately warm up to them and begin asking questions.

In light of this feedback, I recently reflected on what it truly means to be Canadian and looked to the values ingrained in our democratic system of governance to better understand how others viewed this label. Citizenship and Immigration Canada provides one example of what it means to be a Canadian citizen.

Their website states:

"Citizenship means working together with all other Canadians to build a stronger Canada, and making sure our values, dreams, and goals are reflected in our institutions, laws and relationship with one another."

Ingrained in this definition is a notion of cohesion, the sentiment that we truly value collective action and a belief in the freedom to support and live alongside each other. But what are "our values," which this definition refers to?

Some of these values, embodied in legislation such as our Charter of Rights and Freedoms, include freedom and democracy, multiculturalism, linguistic pluralism, and equality before the law. While I recognize that in many respects Canadian values are not a static concept—but rather an ever-changing, malleable set of ideals reflective of our growing and fluid population—there are certain sets of ideas which we could not envision to be absent in a collective Canadian future. The Canadian Index of Wellbeing, at the University of Waterloo, defines some of the values crucial to many Canadian identities, namely:

1. Freedom
2. Peace
3. Fairness
4. Inclusion
5. Democracy
6. Economic security
7. Sustainability
8. Diversity
9. Equity
10. Health

In reviewing these values, I'm struck by how strongly they align with the principle of kindfulness. We value the freedom to be kind to ourselves, to explore what it truly means to be a human being, and allow others to do the same. We believe firmly that all human beings have a role in society and that fairness and the ability to have a say in the collective governance of our envisioned society is integral to being a citizen. We believe that stability and well-being are complemented by embracing difference. We embrace the vision of a kindful nation.

The late George Woodcock, a Canadian author who was from Winnipeg, stated, "Canada's very nature is contained in the fact that it has as many faces as a Buddhist deity." Living just outside of Toronto, I see this multi-faceted Canada that Woodcock refers to. Canada is the home of diversity. Perhaps taking his statement just a tad deeper, we can use this principle when examining our own psyche as human beings. We all possess a multiplicity of faces and personas, which we wear like a new suit, tailored to fit the situation we perceive ourselves to be in. Just as we can wear the suit of anger, frustration, jealousy, or greed, we can also wear the suit of peace, kindness, and joy.

However, despite these strong values being deeply rooted in our national identity, I believe that where we stand as a nation is at a turning point. Political allegations are emerging, which threaten to undermine democracy globally. The pressures of climate change are being felt around the world, leading to early waves of climate refugees fleeing inhospitable disasters and living conditions. Anti-immigrant sentiments abound and the violent abuse of the sanctity of lives have led to global protests and insecurity. The diagnosis of mental health illnesses, such as major depressive disorder and general anxiety disorder, are increasing in prevalence, with some statistics reporting that one in five Canadians experiences a mental illness or addiction problem in any given year. Sadly, though not shocking given Canada's history, our Indigenous brothers and sisters continue to suffer the lasting impacts of colonialism, with whole communities suffering from intergenerational trauma, lacking basic access to clean water and adequate health care, and quite literally, all this after being the bodies upon which Canada was devastatingly built.

The pressures experienced internally by Indigenous peoples to overcome struggles and injustice are also compounded, as they are influenced by and contribute to systemic issues that are occurring on a global scale. In the World Happiness Report 2023, Canada's ranking fell to thirteenth.

Canada's ranking as the thirteenth happiest country in the world is certainly no small feat, as the countries we are ranked behind have had historically high quality of life rankings. However, given our innate tendency toward kindness, our efforts to build an inclusive and democratic society, and the value we place on human well-being, I firmly believe that we can climb the rankings to become the happiest nation on earth. Inundating ourselves with news articles and following every reputable media outlet might lead us to believe that the world is a rather terrible place to live in. However, when I reflect on my daily lived experience, I'm struck by the small moments of kindness that average Canadians display. I once performed a Buddhist blessings ceremony at a Canadian's couple wedding in Niagara Falls. I shared with the couple some words of wisdom for a happy married life. It seems attendees were inspired and delighted with my presence. After my blessings ceremony, some families came up to me to thank me and asked if I would be willing to share tea with them. This kind gesture made me think of how caring some people can be.

Now, imagine a time when we all include one another in our community and company and extend our kind acts of generosity to one another. It is possible to have a mindful and kind nation. For decades, I had had numerous experiences of many gestures of kindness from fellow Canadians.

Mindfulness: Watering the Seed of Kindness

The seed of kindness is indeed present in our culture. This becomes very striking when we look abroad. When we see the conflicts present on our planet and the atrocities that are still happening today—like recently in Ukraine—we see that the atrocities impact the entire planet. In 1992, Sarajevo was under siege by multiple militant forces. This occurred during the lengthy Bosnian War, which resulted in significant loss of life, bombings, artillery fire, and a significant increase in sheer terror for civilians caught in the midst of this horrendous conflict. The siege of Sarajevo was considered the longest siege of a capital city in modern history. Lewis W. MacKenzie, a retired major general in the Canadian Armed Forces and author, stated while reflecting on the horrors of the Bosnian conflict, "If I could have one wish . . . it would be to dump the entire population of Canada in Sarajevo for about six hours. Perhaps then they'd realize Canada is the best damn country in the world."

However, at this point we're at a juncture where the seeds of kindness have been obscured, buried under several layers of dirt. For some of us, those seeds may have been buried for so long that we forgot where we placed them, or are they still even there? At this crucial juncture, how do we reconcile the tensions we experience, endeavour to lead a wholesome life, and nurture the seeds of kindness?

Much like other seeds, the seeds of kindness require water to sprout. This is where the element of mindfulness comes into play. Mindfulness is like the much-needed water. By blending the practice of mindful awareness and self-reflection with that of kindness, we produce the practice of "kindfulness."

Defining Kindfulness

In early 2016, Phra Visuddhisamvarathera, better-known as Ajahn Brahm, published the book *Kindfulness*. The warm-hearted and jovial abbot of Western Australia's Bodhinyana Monastery is also the spiritual director of the Buddhist Society of Western Australia (BSWA). He is well regarded globally for his calm, kind, and caring demeanour, with which he guides and instructs followers in meditation, and for ability to serve as an endless well of corny jokes. Given the many means with which he can make others smile and laugh, it is fitting then that he inspired us all with the term kindfulness.

So, what is kindfulness? In the simplest of terms, kindfulness is the combination of the two words "kindness" and "mindfulness."

With the many mindfulness instructors that exist and with the varying degrees of expertise available to us, the term "mindfulness" has become a catchy word that is readily available to the masses. We often speak about being "more mindful" at work or when completing daily tasks.

The word "kindfulness" has begun to make its way into mainstream news media as well. While "kindfulness" is a blending of two familiar words—kindness and mindfulness—it is also, in a way, beautiful art. Much like the fine strokes required to master calligraphy or the vision necessary to carve a dazzling display out of ice blocks, living a kindful life requires skill, delicate attention, and tact.

In our fast-paced digital era, we have developed a strong tendency toward goal-oriented actions. For those of us currently pursuing a mindfulness practice, we sometimes treat it like going to the gym to work out or eating a quick bite at home. In a sense, mindfulness has become like a chore or task we do to reap some superficial benefits of calm and relaxation so that we can continue with our busy lives, hopefully with slightly more sanity and competence under our belts. As a result, the art of mindfulness is not as prevalent a medium for the expression of beauty in life as it could be. By bringing the practice of kindness to the forefront of our lives, mindfulness becomes a beautiful dance between awareness and love, compassion and ease. Kindfulness, as it were, builds a fluid, ever-changing, and responsive practice that interacts with the daily experiences and flow of life.

Conversely, there are many of us who want to act in compassionate ways. We tend to give all we have, dedicating our time, effort, and resources—material or otherwise—to lift others out of difficult times. This endless giving can leave us burnt out and feeling emotionally destitute. We feel drained and disenfranchised, endlessly caught in a cycle of extreme kindness, followed by depression and feelings of hopelessness at our inability to fix the problems of the world. Sometimes called "compassion fatigue," this state is not to be confused with trauma, which is outside the scope of this book.

Because of the risk of compassion fatigue, our kindness benefits from wise awareness. There is an age old saying that states: "Compassion without wisdom is like a bird with one wing. It only flies in circles." For example, a child crying out for candy may evoke a compassionate response, which is to give the child candy to soothe their mental anguish. However, wisdom would respond by recognizing that the child cannot have the candy because it could ruin their appetite, lead to obesity, or result in the child being spoiled and thinking they can have anything simply because of want at that moment. Rather than follow our compassionate tendencies to give indiscriminately and fly endlessly in circles, the practice of kindfulness tempers our tendency to give by adding both wisdom and awareness to what we or others need, when we have reached the right time and capacity to act.

Kindfulness, then, is the practice of living a balanced, wholesome, and fulfilling lifestyle that is of benefit to all living beings, both ourselves and others. It is a call to remember that by nature we, as human beings, have a tendency toward kindness.

The seed of kindfulness can be found in every human being. This is an innate characteristic of all of us. However, in order to bring out this quality, to nurture it, and let it grow and produce fruitful benefits to your life and the lives of others, we need to draw it out, highlight it, and give it care and attention. The seed of kindness is watered by mindfulness. In this way, we practise kindfulness.

The Vision of a Way Forward

My vision in sharing this with you, is that you will water your internal seed by practising kindfulness. By being mindful of, and recollecting, the innate kindness that exists inside of you, your life will become a source of inspiration to others.

It may be hard to envision that a practice of kindfulness could have such a profound impact. Yet, history is riddled with examples of the influence kindfulness can have.

In 1933, following the rise of Adolf Hitler and the Nazi party, a Jewish family resolved to escape the increasing anti-Semitism in Nazi-occupied Germany. The family fled to the Netherlands and hid in the annex above the father's offices in Amsterdam. The family was helped into hiding by several colleagues who had worked for the father. Through the kindness, support, and care of others, the family was able to successfully hide in the annex above the office for over two years, with colleagues bringing rations and supplies on a consistent basis. Ultimately, the family was captured and sent to concentration camps where the daughters died; only the father survived. This family was the Frank family. The diary of Anne Frank, one of the deceased daughters, went on to provide one of the most moving stories of attempting to survive the Nazi regime.

What is occasionally forgotten in this tragic story is the presence of kindfulness. The individuals who supported the Frank family for more than two years did so despite the possibility of persecution and death. Hearing of the generosity of others at all costs provides us with inspiration that we, too, can live up to our true potential as humans.

By living up to this potential as individuals, the practice of kindfulness will slowly begin to spread, influencing the lives of those around us and inspiring others to pursue a kindfulness practice of their own. Slowly but surely, like drops filling up a bucket with water, Canada will become a more kindful nation as well. And just as a full bucket overflows as water is added to it, kindfulness will soon overflow, influencing and inspiring other countries.

As you set out on your own personal journey toward kindfulness, you may not believe that a more kindful nation is possible, just yet. Albert Einstein said, "Imagination is more important than knowledge. For knowledge is limited to all we now know and understand, while imagination embraces the entire world, and all there ever will be to know and understand." Where are you now? How far has knowledge gotten us as a society? We have smartphones, electric cars, and endless information at our fingertips, and yet, we haven't attained world peace. In many cases, we haven't even realized internal peace! We've continued to repeat some of history's atrocities. So, for the length of this book, I ask that you suspend your judgment. Temporarily put aside the knowledge that you have accumulated. You can pick it back up later. Heed Albert Einstein's advice, and explore the possibilities that are not constrained by knowledge.

Is it possible to build a kindful nation? Perhaps from where we stand right now, you may be thinking this an unrealistic and lofty goal. However, I have the strong conviction that this can be done. How, you might ask? You begin with one. One moment. One person. One family. One neighbourhood. One community. One town. One city. One province or territory. One country . . . and then go beyond. The following story helps illustrate this.

One Hundred Monkeys

One day, a group of one hundred monkeys, discontent with their current surroundings, decided to embark on a long journey through a desolate wasteland at the behest of whispered rumours that there was a beautiful oasis several miles away. Of course, journeying through the desert is a very dangerous, exhausting, and wearisome feat. There is little food, almost no shelter from the elements, and the very mention of water would be sufficient to make you the laughing stock of the animal kingdom.

After slowly trekking for nearly an entire day, without food or water, these monkeys were so tired. With the monkeys over-come with hunger and thirst, their fur matted with sand, and the occasional monkey fights breaking out accompanied by pained screeches, the descent to madness was imminent. Just then, in the distance, they caught a glimpse of something green! The screeches of anger immediately changed to waves of excitement spreading across the entire group, as some began squealing and banging their fists on the sand. Excitedly, the group rushed towards the direction of the shimmering sight of colour in what was otherwise a bleak and dismal landscape.

As they approached, they realized it was a mango grove—in the middle of the desert! Many mangoes had fallen on the ground, and the monkeys went crazy at the sight of them, hurriedly picking mangoes off the ground and shoving them in their mouths. Some monkeys were even using both hands to pick the mangoes, which to any passerby would have looked like a hilarious circus of juggling monkeys!

The hundredth monkey was the last to arrive. Being the least senior and smallest monkey of the group, she had little authority and was pushed aside and trampled on by the other monkeys as they rushed at their first sight of mangoes. The hundredth monkey got back up, equally hungry and thirsty, but now in pain and aching all over. Despite being the smallest, wimpiest, and least imposing of the group, the hundredth monkey had something the others didn't—she was very patient, careful, and observant.

Having grown up in a large family of monkey siblings where she was the last in line, she was often the last to eat. She slowly observed the situation, looking around and getting a lay of the land. She noticed a small clear pond next to the mango tree, which sparked her interest.

She approached the tree and grabbed a half-eaten mango off the ground. She tried it and noticed the mango was tasty, but was mixed with sand and dirt. The grainy texture made for a somewhat unpleasant taste. Recollecting the pond of water just a few feet away, the hundredth monkey decided to wash the next mango she picked up in the pond to see how it would taste. After thoroughly cleaning the mango, she took a bite. Wow! She was suddenly filled with a feeling of deep content at the taste of the juicy, clean, grain-free mango. Delicious! Filled with much joy, she decided to announce her discovery to her fellow monkeys.

She climbed to the top of the nearest sand dune and shouted out (in monkey language, of course), "Hey everyone! Listen up!" A few monkeys turned their heads in mild curiosity, some gave no more than a disinterested glance, however, the rest didn't even budge, too engrossed in their sandy mangoes.

"Guess what! I've discovered a new and delicious taste! It's a sand-free mango! I washed the mango in that pond nearby, and I was able to eat it without dirt and sand. It was absolute bliss— come with me and try it!"

A pond . . . water . . . washing? The few monkeys that had decided to half-heartedly listen to the hundredth monkey were not impressed. Some chuckles arose, eventually growing in decibel until it had turned into outright laughter. What a sight to see— ninety-nine monkeys rolling around in the sand laughing so hard their lungs might burst. The hundredth monkey remained stoic and unperturbed, calling out one last time, "This is a new taste I've discovered. If you wish, try it. If not, so be it." Determined, she continued to gather and wash mangoes in the crystal-clear pond.

The laughter slowly subsided as the monkeys returned to eating their dusty mangoes and grooming each other. Yet, as they clambered off, one monkey remained. The ninety-ninth monkey was standing, gazing at the hundredth monkey, feeling a small glimmer of hope that there might be some truth to the hundredth monkey's madness. The taste of gritty sand was fresh in his mouth, drying out his tongue. Maybe, just maybe, this crazy hundredth monkey was on to something, he thought. Slowly, he picked up a mango off the ground and hobbled over to the nearby pond. He timidly dipped the mango into the water, pulling out what now appeared to be a fresh, glistening golden orb. Just the sight alone made this ninety-ninth monkey salivate. As the hundredth monkey looked on with joy, the ninety-ninth monkey eagerly dove face first into this mango, emerging several moments later with bits of juicy mango barely concealing his grin. The ninety-ninth monkey had tasted the delicious bliss of a freshly washed mango. He was sold!

It wasn't long before both the hundredth and ninety-ninth monkeys were preaching the gospel of a washed mango. It took *a bit of time, but before long, the ninety-eighth monkey was on board. With the other monkeys seeing the crazy monkey trio talking about this new technique of eating a mango, several others decided to cave and give it a shot. You can appreciate that with this kind of momentum building, it wasn't long before the whole group of a hundred monkeys had taken up the new practice of washing mangoes before eating them.*

The hundred monkeys had started on their journey with hopes of finding an oasis. We also are at the cusp of embarking on our own journey as a nation. This is a journey toward the oasis created by kindfulness. We may not entirely believe it to be there yet, but we still have hope, which is why we have the principles of kindfulness so deeply ingrained in our values. We now have a choice to make. Do we stay home or do we take the daring risk of facing the harshness of our own internal struggles so that we come through to the other side and bask in the bliss of kindfulness?

Just as the monkeys in the story readily ate sand-covered mangoes and were reluctant to try washed mangoes, we too are still trying to build a peaceful nation with old methods. And just as the hope for something better led to the entire group of monkeys washing their mangoes, starting with just one monkey, we too can build a kindful nation, starting with just one person. It will not be an easy process and it will require the curiosity, patience, compassion, and resolve of the hundredth monkey in the story. However, by starting with just one person, a kindful nation can be built.

You, who are reading this book now, must consider the following:

How do you live a wholesome life that will better Canada? My vision is that you will be the first seed of kindfulness. If the seed of kindness and mindfulness can grow out of just one person, that one kindful citizen can build one kindful family. These kindful families will produce the next generation of kindful children and leaders, kindful schools and neighbourhoods, a kindful prime minister and kindful provincial premiers. Just like the hundred monkeys, one kindful community can inspire a hundred kindful communities. One kindful nation can inspire a hundred kindful nations. A hundred kindful nations can inspire the world.

Mindfulness allows our innate seed of kindness to grow. Through both mindfulness and kindness, we practise kindfulness. It is this practice of kindfulness that allows us to live up to our greatest potential as human beings. By becoming kindful citizens, we can fulfil the vision of a kindful world. This starts with just one person—you!

Why Develop a Practice of Kindfulness?

Why should we start to develop a practice of kindfulness? Developments in neuroscience over the past decade are providing strong support for the notion that kindness can be developed and that it can have positive effects on ourselves and others. There is now a growing body of evidence demonstrating how receiving kindness and compassion can have positive impacts when healing the body. What may at first sound like conjecture is now becoming a body of science backed by many physicians worldwide. Being the recipient of kindness leads to a release of oxytocin, or the "love hormone," in the brain, which stimulates nitrogen, antioxidants, and anti-inflammatory effects. In other words, when others are kind to us, we feel joy and our body, in turn, stimulates the biological processes necessary to keep us physically healthy.

If the impact our kindness has on others isn't motivation enough, there are also many benefits of a kindful practice on ourselves to help support the cause. Neuroendocrine studies show that consistent loving-kindness and compassion meditation reduce our stress-induced fight or flight response and enhance brain activity in the regions responsible for emotional processing and empathy. Furthermore, actively practising compassion-based therapies is proving to be one of the most effective clinical means of combating chronic depression.[i] New research into epigenetics—the study of hereditary modifications to DNA sequences—is even providing evidence that meditative practices can help heal inherited intergenerational trauma.[ii]

Indeed, the effects of building a practice of kindness into our lives is so powerful that the health-care profession is now incorporating kindness education strategies into training for nurses, with evidence showing that caring could be the difference between life and death.

On a more subjective level, the recipients of kindness are often overcome with the sentiment of "paying-it-forward." They are so moved by the joy that unexpected acts of kindness produce, that they are motivated to perform good deeds for others, both within and outside their normal social circles. Much like the 100 monkeys discussed earlier in this chapter, kindness is contagious. If you are ready to embark on this virtuous path, then it's time to consider how we can develop the performative art of kindness.

CHAPTER 2

Understanding the Journey

"A goal without a plan is just a wish."

— Antoine de Saint-Exupéry

Let me set the stage for this chapter by telling you a story.

The Quest for Happiness

Not long ago, there was a man who left his comfortable home in the middle of the crowded city to depart on a journey. This man was plagued with the incessant gnawing of a thought in the back of his mind that wouldn't leave him alone. "What is the meaning of this life?" This man left his home on a journey to find the answer to this question. A journey to search for the true meaning of life.

His journeys took him around the world, and he encountered people from all walks of life. He consulted with Indigenous knowledge keepers in Canada, philosophers in Greece, traditional healers in South Africa, Zen masters in Japan and spiritual gurus in India. He spoke at length with great imams, rabbis, priests, and monks. He courted the attention and wisdom of respected leaders, authors, poets, artists, CEO's and changemakers. Everyone gave him a piece of what they thought the true meaning of life was, and how to find it. Unfortunately, this man was not convinced. The more information he filled his head with, the further his heart felt from the truth.

He kept searching and eventually wandered into a remote village in an obscure part of Thailand which was at the edge of a mountain and covered by dense jungle thickets. There he heard a rumour of an old wise woman that had been around for as long as the villagers could remember. Not a single soul knew her age, but all referred to her simply as "Ma." Rumour had it that Ma had supposedly found the answer to the meaning of life. After having been on such a fruitless journey for nearly a year now, our unsung hero had become quite sceptical that the answer to his question could be found. Nevertheless, the village residents spoke of Ma with such awe and reverence, that he figured it may be worth a shot. The man decided to purchase some local tea, filled two mugs, and took a long walk to the end of the village where Ma's house resided. Knocking gently on the door, he waited. After a brief pause, the sound of shuffling footsteps, and the creek of a turning lock, an elderly woman with wrinkled, sun-weathered skin that bore a distinct leathery texture answered the door. "Ma?" he asked unsurely. She nodded and motioned for him to come in.

After offering her the second mug of tea, the pair sat in silence for several minutes. Finally, the man couldn't contain his eagerness any longer, and blurted out "I have a question!" Ma gave a knowing nod, as if she had already foretold this. The man asked "I've heard you found the meaning of life. I've been searching for nearly a year, travelling the world and speaking with everyone and anyone that seems to have some fragment of wisdom. And yet, I've found nothing. Please . . . please tell me how I can find the meaning of life" he asked, a hint of desperation filling his voice. Ma sat silently for a while, surveying him as if to judge whether he was indeed worthy of her wisdom. After what felt like hours to the man, but in reality may have been mere seconds, Ma replied by slowly raising her hand, her twisted finger pointing out the window to her left. The man peered out of the window, noticing the peak of the nearby mountain, covered in jungle thickets. Ma spoke, for the first time, which nearly startled the man given the long silence. "There is a cave in the mountain. Nestled deep in the jungle. The cave has a lion shaped mouth. We call it the Lion's Roar. Inside the Lion's Roar there is an ancient well. When it is asked a question, the answer you're looking for will be produced from within."

Though the man was a bit skeptical, a small space in his heart held out some hope that this might just work. After the peculiarities he had encountered along his journey, a talking well certainly was not the strangest thing he had heard about. After all, Ma had the respect of the entire village, and seemed forthcoming.

Deciding to call it a night and head out bright and early in the morning, the man thanked Ma for her time, to which she curtly nodded, then he returned to his guest house at the edge of the village. He prepared his rations and equipment for the hike, then retired for the evening. The man remained restless that night, tossing and turning with barely a wink of sleep. All he could do was ruminate about the possibility of what he might find out when he reached the ancient well.

The next morning at the crack of dawn, when there was sufficient light to see, the man began the arduous trek up the mountain. What started as a gradual, scenic, and quite enjoyable hike, eventually ascended into a treacherous and gruelling feat. His arms and legs got covered in scratches and cuts, as he fought his way through vines and branches. When the dense thicket finally gave way to open air, he breathed a sigh of relief, only to quickly realize the shade of the forest was now gone, replaced instead by the scorching heat of the midday sun. As he continued on, he became drenched in sweat. His legs felt weak, and his breath became shallow and laborious as the altitude increased. Eager to accomplish his goal, he repeated "left . . . right . . . left . . . right" in his head as he slowly placed one foot in front of the other.

Hours had passed, and the sun was descending from its pinnacle in the sky. The man knew he ought to be nearing his destination soon. He stopped and propped himself down on a hollowed log, fumbling to undo the clasp holding his water bottle to his backpack. With one final tug, he managed to pry the clasp loose, only to drop it and watch it roll a few feet away. He bent over to pick up the cap, when suddenly, at the corner of his eye, he spotted it! There it was, a cave with a lion shaped mouth, just as the old lady had described!

Forgetting about his thirst as quickly as it had come on, he rushed towards the mouth of the cave, pausing for just a brief moment to bask in the glory of his achievement. He let a breeze of cool air flowing out from inside the cave brush against his skin. He rushed in, down a long narrow hallway for what seemed like miles, and yet was merely a few feet. As it grew darker in the cave, he came across a glint of light. Whipping out his flashlight, he turned it on, only to see the reflection of the light shine back upon him. He was here, at the fabled well!

He gazed down into its glimmering teal waters, grinning as his own reflection returned the smile! He took a moment to catch his breath, and was frozen with excitement. After a few moments had passed, he took a deep gasp of air, then shouted his question into the well! "WHAT IS THE WAY TO HAPPINESS?! WHAT IS THE MEANING OF LIFE?!" To his utter amazement, the water rippled ever so slightly, and then a soft, ethereal voice echoed back from the well, "What you're looking for is close by. At the base of the other side of this mountain, there is a small village. At the outskirts of this village, there is an intersection marked by a crooked fig tree. Go to the base of the fig tree, and you will find the answer to your questions. You will find the meaning of life. Your journey will end."

Any scepticism he may have had when first hearing the rumours of the wise well had long since left him like geese, travelling south for the winter. His journey had taken him this far, and he wasn't stopping now! A hike down the mountain would be a breeze compared to his hike up, and he was certain, as crazy as it sounded, that the talking well had the answer. Without so much as a thanks, he bolted out of the cave, grabbing his water bottle, retrieving the clasp, slinging his bag around his shoulder, and practically leaping up the last stretch of the mountain. At the top, he could make out heaps of brown and grey, and little specks of moving colour which undoubtedly was the village at the base of the mountain, just as the ancient well had promised. The man practically flew down the mountain, building momentum, sliding at times and scratching his arms, face and legs, but barely giving these minor inconveniences a second thought.

In a quarter of the time it took him to reach the top, he was at the base of the mountain and could see the main village road no more than a few feet away. The sun had begun to set, and the light was waning. He half-walked, half-ran through the village, dodging children playing and villagers carrying food and supplies. After missing a few turns and having to backtrack a bit, he finally spotted it. The crooked fig tree, standing right there at the corner of a dirt road intersection!

He ran up to the fig tree, then waited patiently. When nothing happened, he whispered to the tree, so as not to look mad to passersby, "Fig tree. The well said to come here for my answer. What is the meaning of life?" He waited, and yet, nothing happened. Growing anxious and impatient, he looked around.

The intersection looked fairly unremarkable, save for three shops at the corner, each of which appeared to specialize in one distinct item for sale.

The first shop was selling nylon strings of all lengths and thickness. The second shop was selling wooden handles, similar to

31

broom handles, and the third, was a purveyor of fine metal knobs of various shapes and sizes.

The man looked around, thinking something must be wrong. This was the right intersection, but he certainly didn't feel any happier, and was no closer to finding the truth. He ran up to one of the shop owners, asking the owner if she had heard of some mystical source of happiness here. The owner couldn't understand, and simply shook her head. The second owner was of no help either, but fortunately when he arrived at the third owner, the owner appeared to understand some basic English. The man asked the owner about the source of happiness, and rambled about a wise well that directed him here. The owner shrugged, saying he had no idea what the man was talking about, and clearly believing that the man had cracked under the pressures of the heat and remote wilderness, or perhaps succumbed to some form of illness from his cuts and bruises.

The man was very unhappy at this point; furiously grabbing his belongings he headed back up to the cave, thinking little of the fact that he hadn't eaten all day and was likely suffering from heat exhaustion. Battling back up the mountain in the darkness was no easy feat. Every rustling and cracking of branches meant the possibility of tigers, snakes or worse. However, the man was so angry that he thought "Whatever. If I die, I die. I'm no closer to the truth, and I can't just sit around. I've travelled for a year and found nothing. I'm going back to the well and demanding an answer. I won't rest until I have it."

By the time he reached the entrance, it was pitch black. The man shone his flashlight into the Lion's Roar, and walked up to the well, shouting at it "You lied! I went to the intersection, and all I could find was string, wood and metal! What is this crap? Tell me the way to happiness! How do I become happy, healthy and peaceful?" Glaring back at him was his own sunken face and sullen expression, his angry voice engaging him in a shouting match with himself as it echoed off the walls of the well and the cave, faintly trailing off. The well remained very quiet. The silence frustrated the man more, but despite his repeated questioning, his efforts were futile.

With a heavy heart, the man left the cave and hiked back to the peak of the mountain, dropping his belongings on the ground. Gazing down the west side of the mountain at the second village, he saw lights from torches and lamps. He figured he might as well head back down the mountain and spend the night in this newly encountered village for a change of scenery. He grabbed his things and hurried down to the second village to look for shelter for the night.

Arriving at the base of the mountain, the man wandered through the village looking for a place to stay. As he wandered hopelessly, he passed by the intersection with the fig tree and the three vendors. Weary from his long day of fruitless endeavours, he sat down under the fig tree to take a break, and resolved to just let himself rest for a few moments. Suddenly, he heard the most beautiful, melodious sound he had ever heard. The sound was so beautiful, it caused him to freeze right where he sat. His mind was absorbed by the beauty of the music coming from just a few feet away. He slowly opened his eyes, and looked around, noticing that the sound was coming from just beyond the three shops.

As he approached, the sound got louder and louder, reaching a crescendo and warming him to his core. Finally, he reached the source, and his heart brimmed with joy, bursting through and bringing tears to his eyes, down and over his sheepish smile. There he saw a local musician playing a handmade guitar. The most beautiful sounding guitar he had ever seen or heard, crafted with love and care, neatly polished, and made from three simple ingredients. Wood, string, and metal. The lone wanderer had awakened to his happiness.

Making Music with the Ingredients of Happiness

The ingredients for all that we are looking to create are already present. However, what we desire doesn't come merely from one element. Every ingredient possesses the power to produce the most beautiful music, but they must all work harmoniously, be finely tuned, and played correctly and with skill.

Similarly, in our quest for happiness, there is a process involved so that we may recognize wood, string, and metal for what they are. Just as the man had a set intention to find happiness and set off on a long journey to do so, we too must have the intention to want to be kind, mindful, and happy. Sometimes we don't want these things for ourselves. We may have made decisions in life that we aren't particularly proud of and developed guilt around them. We can feel like we don't deserve to be happy and should suffer. This can lead us to particularly dark mental states. However, no matter where we stand right now, if we set the intention that we wish to be happy, we will have taken the first step on our journey to happiness.

Starting our journey requires having both the belief or view that some form of happiness is possible and that we have the intention to seek that out. Recognizing that there is a better way, we begin on this path by holding that view, which is supplemented by a degree of faith or confidence that the practice of kindfulness can lead us to experience true happiness. This requires a belief that is supplemented by wise reflections, such as the effects our intentions, attitudes, thoughts, speech, and actions have on the overall state of our mental peace, rather than blind or dogmatic faith.

Just as the man in the story had guides along the way in the form of Ma and the well in the Lion's Roar, we too require roadmaps to help us along our spiritual journey. This can be wise teachers, good friends who keep us in check, or the wisdom of elders.

To adequately reflect from a place that is clear and calm, we have to set boundaries on our speech and actions, and live wholesomely, so that we behave and carry ourselves in a way that can assist us to reflect. This is just like the wanderer setting out a plan for his journey. The responsibility we take over our speech, actions, and livelihood serves as the guide for our practice of kindfulness.

Throughout his journey, the lone wanderer had to exert a great deal of effort. He had to hike for hours in treacherous and trying conditions not knowing with certainty whether his goal would even be attainable. To reach our goal, we too must walk onwards, not through forcefulness, but with patient and measured determination. The wanderer had to constantly be mindful of his goal, recollecting it at all times, and returning to it as a source of inspiration. Finally, just as the wanderer had to allow himself a moment of stillness before coming upon the beauty he was searching for, our practice must lead us to internal stillness. From this place of stillness, we can find true happiness.

The Roots of Kindfulness

The practice we are discussing can be likened to a great tree. For a moment, envision an enormous tree. A tree so large, that its branches stretch outward to the Atlantic Ocean to the east, the Pacific Ocean to the west, the Arctic Ocean to the north, and the border to the south, a tree that provides shade to all of Canada. This tree is supported by three main roots, which provide integral structure and support to hold up such a mass. The roots are, in turn, supported by an intricate network of taproots, or feeder roots, which funnel vital nutrients to help ensure the longevity of this ancient tree.

This is the Kindful Tree. The tree of kindfulness has the capacity to support the entire country by providing sustenance and protection from fear, hatred, and anger. It can eradicate racism and bigotry and connect people. This tree can unite, rather than divide, and provide space for joy and happiness under the cool shade of its leaves. The Kindful Tree is a product of humanity. This tree is not tied to any religion, caste, or creed. It is not an artificial construct like race or gender or iPhones and YouTube. Rather, it is the natural awakening of our humanistic nature. Just as the guitar required the three elements of metal, wood, and strings, so too this tree is dependent upon its three roots. Those three roots represent Wisdom, Relationships, and Awareness. Each of the respective roots are supported by smaller feeder or taproots. Wisdom is supported by Kind Perspective and Kind Intention. Relationship is supported by Kind Speech, Kind Action, and Kind Livelihood. Finally, Awareness is supported by Kind Effort, Kind Mindfulness, and Kind Stillness. Together these eight feeder roots—or taproots—support the three main roots, allowing the Kindful Tree to flourish.

Kind perspective is being attuned to the cause-and-effect relationship between your thoughts, intentions, speech, and actions. It's being able to contextualize your relationship to the world and having confidence that sowing positive seeds will reap beneficial fruit. Kind intention is predicated on kind perspective and is a determination to be a source of joy and happiness for yourself and others.

Maintaining this perspective and having the intention to then put it into effect, kind speech, kind action, and kind livelihood blossom and become the manifestation of this kind perspective and kind intention.

Kind effort is the application of attention and energy in a balanced manner. It is not about striving from force, nor being lazy or lax, but coming from an attuned application of the energy and awareness that is necessary to live a balanced life. Kind mindfulness is applying this energy or effort toward wakefulness and relaxed attention. Just as kind intention is predicated on kind perspective, kind mindfulness too is firmly established in the previous roots. Living, speaking, and acting in ways that are kind allow us to have the inner balance and self-confidence necessary to be attuned and wakeful to our inner and outer world.

Finally, kind stillness is the manifestation of the above listed roots. It is the ability to rest gently in the present moment, at peace with whatever the worldly winds of life bring our way. It is the ability to be deeply at peace with oneself and the world around you, irrespective of what comes your way. Each of these concepts will be explored in greater detail in Chapter 13.

Just as the traveller's journey up the hill was steep and treacherous at times, we too will face obstacles in life and difficulties along the way. There will be moments where we think we just can't go any further. There will be trying times when we think kindness toward the "other" simply is not an option. However, these moments will also provide fruitful opportunities to understand what our true potential is and overcome difficulties with grace, humility, and love.

Once the traveller had the roadmap in place, he had to walk the path. No one else could hike the mountain for him. Having the intention in place to be happy but not actually doing anything about it is like being sick; it's like having the medicine to cure your sickness and deciding not to take it. We must take the first steps toward building the Kindful Tree we wish to see covering our nation.

As we embark on our journey toward building a kindful world, we must remember the eight roots that support and sustain our Kindful Tree. These roots work in tandem and should be reflected on frequently, as their meaning will increase in depth as a mirror image to our deepening practice of kindfulness.

CHAPTER 3

The Art of Kindness

"Kindness in words creates confidence. Kindness in thinking creates profoundness. Kindness in giving creates love."

— LAO TZU

If you've made it this far, then you already have the view that happiness is attainable, or at the very least, a sense that the practice of kindfulness can be of some value. You may still be unsure of how far this path can go, yet you have some sense of belief accompanied by a wholesome intention.

To begin our journey toward building this kindful world, we must appreciate the value of making transformative changes to our current lifestyle. Certain parts of our lifestyle may continue to serve us well, while others are traces from a time when we may have needed them but we no longer do. To make these transformative changes, we require an understanding of the dead weight we are carrying around.

To gain this understanding, we must do what the wise Jedi master, Yoda, once said: "You must unlearn what you have learned." This is a key lesson that many prominent artists learn to do, to unlearn what they have learned. Only after throwing out some of the old unused knowledge are they able to develop their own unique style. Much like any skill, the art of kindfulness requires repetitive practice, combined with selective unlearning.

Performing Kindness: Balanced Effort

As human beings, we all possess an innate desire to act in a way that is positive and beneficial, whether to ourselves or, more altruistically, to others. Seeing that we all have this capacity toward goodness, we may feel like we do not need to learn more about how to be kind. Perhaps you may feel that you are already kind enough or that increasing your kindness will serve no practical benefit for you. You may also feel that we are kind enough, given that we live in a culture of "please" and "thank-you." However, what I have observed over my time as a monk is that it can be very easy to take kindness for granted. We can grow complacent with the way we interact with others. Many city dwellers report feelings of isolation or loneliness, despite the Canadian culture of kindness. Operating under the assumption that we do not benefit from being kind to others, especially others who have wronged us, can lead to us developing a degree of rigidity and unfriendliness in our demeanour. Consequently, we become more fragile, lose emotional resilience, and experience loneliness as our lives progress.

To prevent us from becoming unhappy and isolated, we must develop and spread our kindness toward everybody, even those who we may dislike and who may dislike us. It is important to state that this does not mean we become a doormat, allowing others to take advantage of us. Rather, we learn to balance kindness to ourselves with kindness to others, staying attuned to what is required to nurture relationships. Sometimes, this will necessitate communicating clear boundaries and setting limits on what we will condone. Other times, this means being willing to endure difficulties and conflict. However, what it never entails is compromising our ability to retain goodwill toward the human nature of all people, even when we might disagree with and condemn their actions. In other words, we blame the wrongdoing, never the person.

The quality of patient endurance can be seen daily in the majority of us, as we work to earn a living so that we can feel safe, secure, and provide for those whom we dearly love. This desire to create positive benefits in our lives may force us into difficult situations, such as unpleasant bosses. However, we put up with these inconvenient occurrences out of compassion for our family or for financial stability so that we and our loved ones can experience certain comforts. Though this can be uncomfortable at times, by being kind to our loved ones, we are making them and ourselves happy.

It is this desire to be happy that causes some people to be misled into believing that kindness is not the key to true happiness. Thus, with this misguided view, these humans commit violent actions, get addicted to illicit drugs, cheat on their partners, or engage in other negative activities. This mistaken view could lead some to believe that their actions would lead to happiness or that it would ease the negative emotions that disturb their peace. They may seem to gain some comfort or ease in understanding that there is another person to inflict harm upon, or they may feel like they are accepted after fitting in with the wrong crowd. Yet, by becoming attached to these misguided actions, people who feel like they gained happiness from conducting them, in truth, are not happy. This train of thought leads to seeking out temporary relief from psychological pain, at the expense of long-term welfare. Oftentimes, those who repeat these patterns know they are committing harm to themselves, but they do so because they feel they are unworthy of love or kindness, perhaps owing to some childhood trauma.

Imagine if these people received the beautiful gift of kindness and learned to believe that they deserve it. Imagine the beauty they could create.

As mentioned earlier, kindness, much like mindfulness, is a practice or art. Consider the case of an aspiring tattoo artist. Though the tattoo artist may possess the innate talent and interest necessary to become successful, they must still learn the technique and precision required to impress a willing participant. Without the appropriate technique, it is more likely the tattoo artwork will end up an inky blob, and the client will be quite unhappy for years to come.

Similarly, although we possess the inherent potential for kindness, this kindness requires us to develop it into a performative practice and create certain conditions for it to grow to the peak of its potential. Otherwise, we can end up grasping needlessly in the dark, at times successfully creating masterpieces, while at other times, leaving us and people around us hurt and unhappy.

The following ancient story is applicable to everyone embarking on their journey towards nurturing their inner kindness.

The Pair of Acrobats

There were a pair of performing acrobats. One was a senior acrobat, while the other was a more junior assistant who was just getting to know the ropes. The acrobatic duo had developed a unique show, incorporated daring contortions and death-defying flips from immense heights, without the use of safety equipment.

After several years of performing, the acrobatic duo had gained a reputation in their hometown, and decided it was time to move on to bigger things. Luck would have it that they heard about a travelling circus, Cirque de la Nuit, which happened to be holding auditions for a new act. The theme: mindfully silent acrobats! Although it may not sound particularly interesting, the sight of completely silent, peaceful acrobats was an act that had garnered much acclaim! The duo was particularly adept at quietly performing death defying feats, and felt this would be the perfect venue to showcase their skills. Perhaps they may even begin to rake in the big bucks!

With this goal in mind, the duo began practising for their big performance, an act that was sure to amaze and astonish the judges as well as earn them a spot with the travelling circus. Their routine began by building up to a heightened crescendo with various micro-routines, then the novice acrobat would balance on a tiny metal pole, supported by the more experienced master, while both performed individual flips and twirls.

On the morning of the big day, the pair met to regroup and make any final necessary adjustments. "We've put in countless hours and done everything we can to prepare. We just have to deliver now! Remember, climb on my shoulders, and once you're up there, watch what I'm doing and adjust accordingly," said the master. "While you're up there performing your part, I'll stay down here and adjust my moves accordingly to match what you're doing. Our routine will be sure to impress!"

The apprentice gave the master a puzzled look. "What?" said the master. "Master, it doesn't work that way, though! You're on the ground providing the base for everything I do. You have to take care of yourself first, and then I'll be able to take care of myself. By each of us looking after our own routine, we'll provide the support and coordination for the other person," replied the young apprentice.

It turns out the master stood to learn a thing or two from his young apprentice. Rather than trying to take their cues by constantly observing each other, the act benefitted by each mastering their own abilities and skills, and they performed to perfection. It goes without saying that the dazzling performance left the judges in awe, and secured them a spot in the travelling Cirque de la Nuit.

A Symbiotic Relationship

Interdependence was at the core of the acrobatic duo's success. Neither acrobat could have impressed the expert judges individually. They required each other throughout the routine. And yet, in order to honour each other's performance fully and work harmoniously, they had to ensure they mastered their individual abilities.

Much like the acrobatic duo, this concept of interdependence can be applied to most social systems. We are inherently reliant on each other and can often overlook the ways in which we are required to trust others to perform their part. Consider going out to the convenience store to pick up a carton of milk. Along the way, you trust that no one else will inflict harm on you. You trust that when you arrive at the store, the owner will have done his part in ensuring that the milk was ordered, stocked, and maintained. Your dependency extends to the farmer who raised the cow and produced the milk, the truck driver who transported it, and even the company profiting from its sale for making the entire process possible.

We, in turn, as individuals, honour this interdependence by looking out for ourselves. By caring for ourselves, we in turn care for others. Take marriage as an example. How happy will your partner be if you are unhappy? If one partner is unhappy, the other partner is unhappy as well. If you suddenly stopped grooming yourself, doing things that made you happy, and let yourself slip into a state of depression, your partner would quickly begin to suffer as well from your inability to care for yourself. They might attempt to care for you, which is certainly very noble and kind, but if you made no effort, they would quickly become emotionally exhausted and the entire relationship would dissolve.

The same process applies to all forms of relationships. If the parents aren't happy, the kids won't be happy and vice versa. Many unhappy bosses and CEOs create suffering for their employees. The repercussions of not being happy with yourself may not always present themselves immediately, but discontent festers over time. Many people who engage in work in the health-care sectors, social services, the legal profession, or other service-oriented professions frequently report feeling burnt out at various points in their career. This, in turn, can affect their personal lives and health. Indeed, for many caregiving professions, the requirement for self-care is viewed not simply as a luxury, but as an ethical requirement of the profession in order to avoid negatively impacting clients and care receivers.

If we become discontented, this feeds into all of our relationships and makes us a source of discontentment for others. If we seek to make ourselves happier through caring for ourselves, we become a source of joy for others. By caring for ourselves, we care for others.

I frequently counsel people who feel burnt out by their giving. They volunteer all their time, do anything that anyone asks of them, run errands, donate money, or arrange and plan events. They pour their energy into helping others and eventually feel they can no longer give; they feel fed up with the world. This relates to the saying I mentioned earlier: "Compassion without wisdom is like a bird with one wing. It only flies in circles."

Now, you might be saying, "Isn't it selfish to just focus on myself?" If indiscriminately giving without reflecting on your own needs is one extreme to be avoided, developing a selfish view that only considers your own wants is the another extreme. It is also quite important to not confuse the act of self-care with self-centredness. Without constant reflection on your intentions in any given interaction, you may begin to neglect people under the pretense of caring for yourself. By reflecting on and exploring the interactions in our relationships, we gain a more realistic appreciation of how life operates and a healthier decision-making capacity. Consistently practising to develop a deep, inner awareness will allow us to understand our motivations and intentions at all times and provide us with the wisdom necessary to reflect on how we relate.

Just as we care for others by caring for ourselves, the opposite also holds true. By caring for others, we care for ourselves. I only need to reflect on my own life as a monk to see how caring for others has led to my own well-being. Throughout the years, I have provided counselling services, given emotional support, blessed marriages, performed funeral services, held meditation classes, and provided a safe space for countless individuals. The old adage states that "nothing is free," so perhaps that's why my services are so cheap! I offer "nothing-ness:" spaciousness, acceptance and love, the absence of judgement. As a result of dedicating my life to a practice that entails caring for the well-being of all sentient life forms, I have seen the resulting happiness and received immeasurable support in return. The support of lay followers has led to having a roof over my head, robes to clothe myself, satiating food, and lifelong friends.

Seeing the happiness instilled in others also produces joy in our own hearts. Meanwhile, our minds begin to gravitate toward a deeper state of peace, as we naturally let go of some of the anxiety and fear of being harmed or taken advantage of. We lean more toward an emotional openness because we begin to trust in the merit of our own good deeds. We know that others won't hurt us because we have done good for others and, in turn, they know we won't hurt them. A natural peace comes from the symbiotic relationship of caring for others, and this natural peace makes the practice of developing a deep inner awareness possible.

This is not to say that we will never get hurt. However, much of the fear and worries that lead to us becoming emotionally closed fade away because we recognize our good actions will produce more positive benefits than harm. Therefore, the few times we may get taken advantage of or hurt become minor speed bumps in the grand scheme of the journey toward a happier life. In other words, our kindness builds emotional resilience.

To summarize, we can see how kindness—and the practice of simultaneously caring for ourselves and others—is supported by, and, in turn, supports mindfulness. That is to say, just as the relationship of kindness between self and other is connected so is the relationship between kindness and mindfulness similarly connected. Thus, the practice of kindfulness is a performative art which should be undertaken repeatedly, with care and diligence.

Part Two

You and Others

CHAPTER 4

Caring for Yourself: Three Steps

"It's not selfish to love yourself, take care of yourself, and to make your happiness a priority. It's necessary."

— MANDY HALE

In this chapter we will explore how kindfulness—be kind and remember not to forget to be kind—begins with caring for yourself. The process that follows consists of a few simple steps that will help you to do that.

Step 1: Identify and Master Existing Qualities

1. Make a list of your best qualities, those you practise on an active basis. Some examples are confidence, mental energy, stillness, humility, compassion, gratitude, self-reflection, acceptance, adaptability, and mindfulness. This is not exhaustive list; feel free to add other qualities you deem important.

2. Consider prioritizing your list in order of importance and for future reference. *who has time for this?!*

3. Choose one quality to begin with, one you wish to develop or one you wish to improve upon or master

more effectively. You will find you will improve if you act mindfully.

4. Make a list of new actions or activities you will take to enhance this quality, including small actions and activities.

As you work through your list you may want to update it periodically, as qualities diminish or improve due to circumstances, situation, and life events.

Step 2: Identify and Cultivate New Qualities

Suppose a busy investment advisor decides to leave his position to start a farm. In order to succeed, he will have to assess his resources and invest those resources in the best way possible. Once the resources are invested and the farm is up and running, the new farmer will seek to incorporate, on an ongoing basis, new methods to improve his farm.

1. Make a list of qualities you wish you had. You can refer to the list of qualities in Step One as a starting point, or add those qualities you wish to work on.

2. Consider prioritizing your list in order of importance and for future reference. ??

3. Choose one quality to begin with, one you wish to cultivate. You will find you will develop this new quality if you act mindfully.

4. Choose a mantra—a positive affirmation—consisting of a word or phrase that you will repeat to yourself silently and periodically.

5. For example, with regards to acceptance and adaptability, you may find it helpful to frequently return to your breath throughout the day. When doing so, recite "I am here" when inhaling, and "I am safe" when exhaling. If you find that this gets you caught up in thinking, shorten

your mantra and use a word instead. For example, repeat "peace . . . peace . . . peace." The goal is to avoid reciting a mantra that will send you back into a state of repetitive or negative thinking. Instead, have a reflective way of recognizing when your mind is embodying the qualities you want to cultivate, and recognize when it is being held back. This is not about beating yourself up; think of it as a means to get curious about your experience, to understand first-hand what causes you to struggle or suffer, and how to cultivate opposing qualities that will allow you to overcome your struggles.

6. Make a list of what you can do on a regular basis to put this quality into action.

Step 3: Repeat Habitually

Once you've identified your existing qualities, and identified new qualities you wish to develop, it is important to create habits with concrete actions in order to nurture this development. Just as bad habits can easily form and take over your life, so too can good habits.

When you notice how existing or new qualities are beneficial to your life, identify related actions that produce the desired results. You may notice certain patterns. For example, if inherent joy was on your list of qualities, you may notice that this quality arises when you give something to a stranger without being prompted. You can then follow the chain of causality and notice that giving to others produces joy.

Once identified, it's important to engage in habitual repetition. Continue to give to others. Give not just when you feel inspired, but also when you don't. If you simply repeat the accompanying action only when you feel inspired to do so, you'll develop a weak habit at best, and very soon your momentum will slow and you will lose all the inspiration you once had. Following the whims of your moods and simply doing what you feel like, when you feel like it, can lead you to pursuing highs and experiencing depths of lows. It will leave you scrambling to determine how you can find deep inner happiness. By contrast, engaging in a systematic investigation of the causes of your happiness, and then developing the habit of happiness, holds the potential for a deeply fulfilling life.

For example, when you pass by someone in need and don't feel like helping because you're too busy, you must intentionally go against that thinking and give what you can, be it time, lending a compassionate ear, or material support where you can. In this way, you'll override the animalistic tendencies of stinginess, greed, anger, delusion, ego-centric view, and doubt, and in their place, nurture the positive qualities you are seeking to develop.

One action that will assist you in developing many of the traits you are seeking is loving-kindness meditation. Engaging in a meditative or contemplative practice is one of the most important forms of self-care you can engage in. This does not need to be rooted in a religious, spiritual, or faith-based tradition, but it does need to be consistent and maintained. Just as you exercise on a consistent basis to maintain a healthy body, so too must you take your mind to the gym. At times, you may not like going to the gym, but as you begin to go and see results, you know that the value of being kind to yourself by riding past the discomfort and resistance, and continuing the practice of exercise far outweighs any resistance you may have. Meditation and the resulting stillness produced by meditation are the mind's gym.

In a later section, we will look at techniques of loving-kindness meditation, which you can begin to incorporate into your practice, along with additional forms of kindful meditative techniques to add to your toolbox.

CHAPTER 5

Caring for Others: Four Ways

"Be certain that you do not die without having done something wonderful for humanity."

— MAYA ANGELOU

In this chapter we discuss four ways in which we can care for others.

By caring for others as much as you care for yourself, you nurture a healthy relationship with the world; for it is through caring for others that you also care for yourself. The two are interdependent. Here are four ways to care for yourself by caring for others.

Practise Acceptance

It is what it is. Acceptance is the ability to be present with the ups and downs of life. It does not mean that you will always like the outcome of everything, nor that you have to pretend to like the way things are when you do not. Rather, it means that you recognize what is in your control and what is not. Opening yourself to reality makes you flow naturally with life;

it allows you to appreciate what is, to be present to the delicate and fleeting nature of your surroundings, and to let go of things when the time comes. This cultivates an inner security that isn't dependent on perfect conditions that last forever. You appreciate and enjoy the changes that life brings, not looking and seeking them out, but not oppressing them when they arrive either. You develop a state of deep inner self-confidence where you trust that you can take on any of life's challenges.

This outlook should not be mistaken for passive acceptance. You don't simply wash your hands of responsibility and obligation. Rather than setting unrealistic demands on life, you recognize the opportunity to act in a way that creates positive change. You also recognize when to step back and allow life to take its course. You grow past the fear and uncertainty and mature into a person who is able to live life fully and wholeheartedly. Adopting an attitude of acceptance also means you can love fully. You learn to accept others as they enter and leave your life naturally. In this way, you care for yourself by caring for others.

This is exactly what you are instructed to do when on a plane in an emergency. First, you check that you are OK. Once you have your own oxygen mask on, you are then in a position to help others.

Thomas Anthony Harris states in his book *I'm OK-You're OK* that there are four life positions that each of us takes:

> I'm OK, you're not OK.
> I'm not OK, you're OK.
> I'm not OK, you're not OK.
> I'm OK, you're OK.

In the era of social media, where we see images of other people leading what appears to be a perfect life with a perfect body, a beautiful partner, great kids, wealth, and success, it's easy to understand why "I'm not OK, you're OK" is the most common position taken.

There needs to be a shift to the position "I'm OK, you're OK."

Commit to Harmlessness

"There are many causes I would die for. There is not a single cause I would kill for."

— Mahatma Gandhi

A commitment to harmlessness—to refrain from causing harm—is a signal to other sentient beings that they are safe in your presence. When you enter your comfortable home, you'll notice that your perception and feelings shift. Your shoulders start to relax and you start releasing the stress of the day. This is because you have reached your safe place, where you are accepted and don't have to worry so much about surviving or being harmed. When you commit to harmlessness, you commit to being the safe place for other living things. Those who enter your presence begin to feel a certain degree of comfort and they too can begin to let their guard down.

Harmlessness extends beyond refraining from physically harming a living being to refraining from emotional harm as well. Gossiping, criticizing, or belittling can all be harmful and divisive. When you refrain from actions, speech, and thoughts that could create physical or emotional harm to another being, you signal that you are committed to harmlessness, that you are friend, not foe. You begin to attract into your life others who value peace, safety, and supportive relationships. Through this attitude and practice of harmlessness, you reduce your sense of isolation and egocentrism and feel a greater sense of unity with the world.

Practise Empathy

"So what is empathy? It's the ability to understand another person's thoughts and feelings in a situation from their point of view, rather than your own. It differs from sympathy, where one is moved by the thoughts and feelings of another but maintains an emotional distance."

— BRENÉ BROWN

Well-respected author Brené Brown draws a distinction between sympathy and empathy by saying, "Empathy fuels connection. Sympathy drives disconnection."

Sympathy can be described as feeling a sense of sorrow, pity, or sadness for another living being. In contrast, empathy is the emotional act of "putting yourself in the shoes of another" — taking on what they feel and sharing their perspective so that you can try to understand what they are going through.

To understand why sympathy can drive disconnection, think back to a time when you were going through some difficulties. You opened up to someone only to be met with statements such as, "That sucks" or "I feel sorry for you." Do you feel better?

In contrast, you may recollect a time when you were vulnerable with someone close to you and they listened wholeheartedly. They connected with you through their body language, patience, and attentiveness. They gave you space to speak and express your frustrations in a non-judgmental way, and communicated their understanding and support. This is empathy.

Being empathetic is not a series of statements or words or an intellectual exercise, but rather it is an emotional response to the suffering of another human being. It is a willingness to connect through shared suffering and respond with humility, to turn toward, rather than away. It may seem quite intuitive how empathizing with another human translates to caring for others. But how does stepping into the emotional space of another human being lead to you caring for yourself?

Social and emotional isolation is one of the most common sentiments among youth in the western world. It is a feeling that has become more pronounced during the shift to a digital world, and more recently during the restrictions and lockdowns brought about by the global pandemic. Despite the increase in connection through the internet and social media, more people are reporting being depressed. While there are many causes, one key factor is an increased sense of social isolation. Empathizing with other human beings transcends the superficial feeling of connection and allows us to truly connect to our human nature. It bypasses the external differences of race, religion, language, and class, cutting to the core of what it means to feel and live as a human with all of the accompanying emotions. Rather than deny the part of us that suffers, we open up and become vulnerable to it, then share that vulnerability with another human being who is also struggling. In other words, practising empathy makes us a more wholesome and complete individual.

How can you develop the emotional intelligence necessary to practise empathy? Here are some pointers:

1. Practise active listening. Maintain eye contact with other people when they speak. Ask non-judgmental and open-ended questions.

2. Be fully present. Hold off on any thoughts and judgment in order to remain in the present moment.

3. Relate your own emotions with care and attention. Know what you're feeling so you can communicate that.

4. Communicate with both facial expressions and body language. Show the person that you are paying attention to them and care about what they are saying.
5. Embrace discomfort. Sometimes being silent and feeling the discomfort that comes with difficult conversations is the best way to show empathy. Silence can be great. Be willing to create a space of silence that acts as a cushion to catch or receive the other person's emotions.
6. Develop a meditative practice around loving-kindness.

Test these skills. The next time someone confides in you, see if you can practise empathizing in this way. Notice how engaging in this practice makes you feel, and pay attention to the impact it has on the person confiding in you. It is not uncommon to find others beginning to express how good a listener you are, or how therapeutic it feels to speak to you. In this manner, you are creating a climate of acceptance. You are beginning the first steps of changing the way you relate to your environment. You are practising the art of kindfulness.

Practise Loving-Kindness ✓

"Kindness trumps everything. Kind people are magnets for all of the good things in life."

— TOM GIAQUINTO

Kindness is an art. We are artists, and life, in all its intricate glories, is our canvas. Begin to reflect on the symbiotic nature of life and all of the ways nurturing both self and others in a balanced manner, while neglecting neither, can produce great joy. Start by picking one loving-kindness practice that speaks to you

from the ways of caring for ourselves and others. As your practice develops, you may begin to notice yourself naturally caring
in many of the other ways outlined above. Loving-kindness may
also be developed further through loving-kindness meditation,
which we will discuss in an upcoming chapter.

CHAPTER 6

The Practice of the Heart

Buddhism

"By the practice of meditation, you will find that you are carrying
within your heart a portable paradise."

— PARAMAHANSA YOGANANDA

Regardless of which meditation technique you use, the important and consistent emphasis is that loving-kindness meditation
is a practice of the heart.

Here, I don't necessarily mean the heart as the beating
organ producing physical sensations in the centre of your chest,
although this is not to preclude physical sensations from being
present when we think of the heart. Rather, when I refer to a
practice as one of "the heart," I refer to the shared perception
of having a core to your emotional experience of the world. For
many of us, this core feeling is physically located in the chest
or abdomen and can be experienced throughout the body. For
others, it may be more cerebral and felt in the head initially,
however, when you begin to learn how to practise loving-
kindness meditation, you move your awareness away from the
cognitive centre down to the emotional centre of your body.
Practising loving-kindness meditation allows you to integrate
your heart, mind, and body to experience what it means to be
a complete human being. This sense of wholeness resides at the

core of your heart. In the ancient Pali language, the word "citta" is used to refer to the totality of mental and emotional processes and is often translated as the "mind/heart."

If you have grown up in a western society, it may be difficult to relate to citta—mind/heart—as you have been conditioned to be quite cerebral. You associate yourself with your brain and have been trained to think in a logical and systematic way. This certainly has its benefits and place, as many daily tasks require this type of thinking and outlook. Scheduled meetings require assessing the importance of the meeting, determining how much time is required to prepare, ensuring relevant deadlines are met, engaging in risk assessment, and reviewing documents. However, it is your over-reliance on this thought process that often leads to neglecting your emotional world, feeling socially isolated, or being unable to adequately process and communicate emotions. It leads you to feeling like the world around you is to blame for your problems.

Developing a perception of the heart is a way to help relate to the emotional element of citta, rather than just the logical and systematic. This perception is one that you can build at any point in the day when something impacts your emotional world. You can map the experience of your emotions with changes in your body temperature, blood flow, heat, and energy throughout your body. It follows that your emotional world is not simply an experience of the head, but also an experience of the body as it interacts with the world. Through loving-kindness, you can learn to understand this world of feeling and being.

To do so, it requires that you pay close attention to your emotional world and how you experience it, both in mind and body. However, if you've ever been overwhelmed with anger, frustration, jealousy, sadness, or anxiety, you know that it can be difficult to have a perspective on these emotions when you're drowning in them. Think, for example, of being caught up in

61

The Practice of the Heart

a fit of rage only to later regret expressing your anger or being lovestruck when dating a new partner, only to discover all of their flaws a few months later. Drowning in your feelings is being unable to gain perspective and see things as they really are.

To circumvent this, start with the easier task of paying attention to your physical experience. When an emotion arises in you, try to notice where you feel it in your body. If you're annoyed, is there tension that comes with that? Where do you notice that tension, and what are its characteristics? Are they the same as anger or different? When sadness strikes, does the temperature in your body change? What about anxiety? What feelings arise in your chest and stomach? As you develop a perception of your physical experience, you strengthen your reflective awareness of the emotional-physical link in the mind. This is the practice of getting to know the heart.

Engaging in this type of practice will prime your perception and awareness for the practice of loving-kindness meditation, and make many of the steps that follow seem intuitive in nature. It may seem tempting to skip over this preliminary step, but it is not recommended. The simple act of getting curious about the mind-body connection is a profound act of loving-kindness. This practice sends a simple message to you. It says to your body and your mind, "I am willing to look and listen to you because I care. I care enough about your well-being to ask, 'How are you right now?'" This is an act of loving-kindness toward yourself.

CHAPTER 7

A Beginner's Guide
to Meditation

"Meditation makes the entire nervous system go into a field of coherence."

—DEEPAK CHOPRA

Mandy –
became incoherent

Once you feel that you have mastered the practice of the heart, you can proceed to loving-kindness meditation. For many, the notion of evoking a sense of loving-kindness can sound esoteric at best or downright impossible. However, it does not need to be.

There are various techniques of loving-kindness meditation. Some practitioners emphasize the use of visual or imaginary objects to evoke feelings of love and compassion. Others advocate for the tried-and-true method of beginning with self-love and radiating it outward until the entire world is enveloped with the warmth of kindness. With any, it is important to be consistent.

v12
Literally

But I don't
love myself

The Four-Step Loving-Kindness Meditation

The following meditation presents a way of building a reflective and contemplative practice. Before you begin:

- Find a quiet and safe space where you can sit without interruption
- Accept and appreciate yourself for setting out this time for practice

Step 1: Evoke the Sensation of Loving-Kindness

In this first step, your intention is to associate a mental or physical feeling with the experience of loving-kindness. Naturally, you can only begin the practice of loving-kindness meditation by understanding what that quality of loving-kindness feels like. You can begin by using your experience of the mind and body as a tool to cultivate loving-kindness.

I recommend you start with a visualization technique. To do this, select a person or object that evokes a sense of joy and happiness in you. You should avoid material possessions, as these can be laden with negative emotions, such as greed. It helps to pick a living or sentient being. Even then, you must not select someone for whom you might have mixed emotions of love and aversion, such as a person you may have fought with recently. You might like the idea of puppies and babies as the most innocent and innately pure expressions of life. Once you've had the opportunity to spend a few minutes or so relaxing your body and settling into a seated position, you can begin.

After selecting who or what to focus your loving-kindness toward, envision that living being in front of you. Spend time conjuring up a detailed image, like the fluffy fur, big watery eyes

64

gazing up at you, and tail slightly wagging. I hope at this point you realize my example is of a dog and not a baby!

Much like all other elements of meditation, it's important not to rush the process. As you envision your warm, cuddly friend in front of you, a sensation of warmth and lightness may begin to appear in you. Notice where this feeling arises and what qualities it has without giving it a name. The sight of a furry friend may cause a warm sensation to bloom in your chest and gradually fill your body.

Once this feeling is fully present, continue to play with this visualization. Imagine yourself slowly and gently bending over to get closer to your friend without disturbing him. To ensure you don't frighten him, you have to move extremely slowly and gracefully in your mind, with the utmost sense of care and attention. As you approach, you notice he edges away slightly, but then begins to grow curious, his small nose wiggling as he sniffs you and approaches. As he gets closer, you ever so gently caress his head with your fingers. These gentle caresses ease his worries, and he begins to nuzzle up to your palm, until you're able to cup him in your hand, pick him up, bring him close to your chest, and feel the warmth of his beating heart pressed against you. The Kitten I had.

If you've picked a family member or close friend, you might wish to imagine walking into a room and seeing them after a long absence. Perhaps the pandemic has kept you apart for some time. When you enter the room, you spot each other. You instantly see their face turn from a neutral expression into a beaming ear-to-ear smile filled with so much love and happiness. That smile, you begin to realize, is a mirror image of your own smile at seeing them, as you notice the corner of your lips rising into a grin with the happiness that fills you. You quickly run to each other to embrace, and you feel the warmth and joy of their body pressed against yours as you hold them.

When you notice that the warm sensation of joy and love is easily present in your body, you can gradually let go of the visualization and become more focused on the physical and mental sensations of loving-kindness. You now have associated loving-kindness with your body and your mind in a way you can readily relate to. It's very important that you do not abandon your visualization too hastily. If shifting your awareness toward the sensation of loving-kindness itself—as opposed to the visualization—creates tension, stress, restlessness, or lack of ease, this is a clear sign that you are trying to force the meditation to progress at a rate faster than nature will allow it.

In addition, do not assume that every time you sit to meditate will be the same. You may get used to shifting your attention toward loving-kindness after a particular amount of time has passed, only to find that the next time you meditate, things take longer. You may also find that you sit down to meditate expecting that it will take a long time to evoke the feeling of loving-kindness, only to find that it immediately springs forth the moment your bottom touches the cushion. This is a very natural process, and it must be allowed to take its own course at the rate that is suitable to each particular moment.

Step 2: Saturate in Loving-Kindness

Once the sensation of loving-kindness is fully present in your mind, focus on growing or strengthening that feeling. While you eventually want to think about projecting loving-kindness toward others, at this stage it may still be too early to do so. If you attempt to move on to other people too quickly, you may notice that your mind begins to notice their faults, which seems to poke holes at what is a rather superficial degree of loving-kindness. Before long, loving-kindness can evolve into your habitual thinking. Alternatively, the planning mind might kick into high gear, thinking about the last time you saw that person and strategizing for the next meetup or coffee date. These distractions take you away from the loving-kindness as a meditation object and cause your meditation to fall apart. You have to cherish the feeling of loving-kindness and prioritize that above all other things at this particular time.

To guard against this pitfall and really solidify your attentive mental state, it's important to spend time immersing yourself in the feeling of loving-kindness. This stage is saturation because it gives you an idea of how pervasive you aim to make this feeling. This not a process that can be forced. Rather, it's your ability to sit with the sensation with ease and acceptance that allows it to really grow in power.

Picture a nice round ball of mozzarella cheese. That cheese is saturated with moisture, porous, and absorbent. If you've ever purchased fresh mozzarella from the grocery store, you will recall that it comes in a container of liquid. When you remove the cheese, it is slightly damp and absorbent. A different image may be a sponge dipped in water. The sponge soaks up water until it's fully saturated.

The practice in this step is to fully soak up the sensation of loving-kindness. Let it fill your entire body and mind—gradually, delicately, and intently—until such time as you're immersed in the feeling. One of the most important parts of this practice is to give yourself love. Once your loving-kindness is strong, it can be quite easy to project it to others. If there is a particularly tense spot in your body, or an illness or injury you have been dealing with for some time, you may want to project your loving-kindness toward that spot. It can help to envision this emotion as a beautiful gold thread or energy, wrapping itself around you and enveloping you with comforting joy. Or if there is a particular worry or fear that has been weighing on you, feel free to experiment with blasting that anxiety or sadness with loving-kindness. You would be surprised how many meditators tell me how loving-kindness has caused their physical pains to lessen, or in some cases, even disappear completely. You are profoundly transforming the way you relate to the stressors of your mind and body.

Even if you were to stop meditating at this point, you would still notice a light, joyous, and relaxed feeling in your body. As you return to your activities, many of the daily stresses may feel temporarily removed and more remote in comparison to the gentle, tangible sensation of loving-kindness. You may notice yourself smiling for no particular reason. People may even comment that your complexion seems lighter or that you've been nicer lately.

As you continue to develop the practice, don't stop here. Gradually continue to immerse your attention in the sensation of love and kindness until you feel it saturate your entire experience. It's at this stage that you can then experiment with directing the flow of this power in several different ways.

Step 3: Spread the Kindness Outward

With love and kindness at its peak, you now have the opportunity to direct its power toward other living beings. Choose someone who is relatively close to you. Starting with a stranger may feel a bit too abstract. For example, choose your mother, father, brother, sister, or someone else you are close to. Starting with this person, imagine that love is like a golden thread or ball of energy, flowing from your heart toward that person. Play with that energy, let it surround and envelop that person from head to toe. If that energy wraps around that person, envision it saturating that person, similar to how you were saturated with energy. As that person becomes filled with that energy, notice how the corner of their lips become wider as they smile, their eyes glistening as they look back at you with love and kindness.

When that person is fully saturated with love and kindness as well, continue to progressively spread this power toward other living beings, like another relative, and eventually to friends, colleagues, and even acquaintances or strangers. Eventually, you can envision this power spreading to all people, irrespective of whether they are friendly, indifferent, or hostile. You can even extend this energy to all living beings, whether they are human or not. You can extend it to animals, plants, insects, or—depending of your beliefs—to ancestors, spiritual beings, or angels. You also can extend it into the heavens, outward to the stars, or downward to the depths of the earth. You can extend this power infinitely, without boundaries, and beyond space and time.

As you become more adept at this practice, you may not even require imagining friends or relatives or any beings in particular. You may be able to evoke the saturated feeling of loving-kindness and then radiate it outward without the use of visualization techniques. You'll eventually have the capacity to do this.

As you play with these perceptions of boundlessness and timelessness, you may notice a strong sense of union. Some people describe this as reaching the place of nothingness or experiencing the love of God, depending on your beliefs. Others call this a sense of unity of being one with the universe. However you describe it, the more important point is that you are now delving into the core of your capacity as a human being. At a psychological level, you are reconditioning your perception of the world. You are removing the conditioning that acts as a barrier to truly perceive the world as it is, in all its beauty. You're beginning to see the world with all its wonders and flaws, and learning to accept and love it regardless.

It's lovable.

* * *

You may carry around regret, guilt, and doubt about decisions you've made or the people you may have harmed. You may sometimes feel that everyone else is worthy of love except you, that you are somehow hopeless or beyond saving. If these feelings prevent you from enveloping yourself with loving-kindness during any of the previous steps, then this is a good time to try.

The goal is to gradually work toward extending loving-kindness to that which you find hardest to love. By the time you get to yourself, to an enemy or the hated other, the momentum of your practice will be so strong that any preconceived notion about who or what is loveable or not will collapse. You will find that loving-kindness is not something you earn through your deeds, but something you are innately deserving of, simply by virtue of the fact that you are here.

I just loved Miss Woolacott

Step 4: Continue the Journey

This step should be cultivated with ease. The gradual practice cannot be controlled, rushed, or manipulated in any way. It should be gentle using balanced effort and attention. When you do eventually reach this final stage, the most important thing to do is to let go. The energy and power of loving-kindness is so strong at this stage that you need to do nothing except get out of the way. The visualizations that you used earlier must now be relinquished. They serve no purpose at this stage as they limit or restrict in some way the true nature of loving-kindness. Let yourself experience that energy directly. That experience has the ability to carry you all the way to enlightenment and true liberation. This final step takes immense courage, as you must be willing to let go fully. When you do, it will be bliss, at last.

People who are full of loving-kindness — the rose specialist in Yogananda's autobiog" Aunty Beat. Luther Burbank (gentle) Nanny Lorna at times re Nicky.

CHAPTER 8

Other Meditation Techniques

"At the end of the day, I can end up just totally wacky, because I've made mountains out of molehills. With meditation, I can keep them as molehills."

— RINGO STARR

After you become proficient with the steps of beginner loving-kindness meditation, you may want to experiment with other techniques. Not every technique suits all people at every stage of their life. However, that should not be an excuse to avoid persisting with a technique, though some techniques may feel more natural at times to you than others. Below are a few alternatives for evoking and playing with the perception of loving-kindness. The word "playing" is used to emphasize the type of attitude you should bring to your meditation practice, an attitude of curious exploration and gentleness, similar to the way a child might play. With that attitude in mind, feel free to try the following techniques:

Breathing in Loving-Kindness

maranatha

Some people find it effective to breathe in loving-kindness. This is particularly helpful if you have difficulty with a visualization technique. Breathing in loving-kindness is exactly what it sounds like. Using the words "loving" and "kindness" as a sort of mantra, recite the two words with each in and out breath. Try mentally reciting "loving" on the in breath and then "kindness" on the out breath, and feel what that does to your body and mind. Alternatively, try inhaling to the word "love" and exhaling to the word "relax." Or breathe in to "love" and out to "peace." Other options are breathing in a positive energy, like "love," and breathing out a negative energy, like "stress." The word itself is not particularly important; what is important is the connection your mind and body have with those words and how those words might evoke sensations you associate with loving-kindness.

Just as with any other form of meditation, you should first spend some time allowing your body to settle in or even doing some body scanning meditation to fully relax your body, rather than jumping straight to breathing. When you gradually settle on your breath, you can begin your selected mantra, such as breathing in "love" and breathing out "kindness." As you consistently follow this pattern, you may notice the breath beginning to get lighter and easier. You should not try to control the breath to make it easy or blame yourself if it doesn't become easy. You haven't done anything wrong. Simply notice the quality of your breath as it changes during the course of your practice. Eventually, you will notice the sensation of loving-kindness arising in you, and you may progress to any of the other steps of this practice.

Healing the Body with Loving-Kindness

The practice of loving-kindness has many practical applications, one of which is that it can have a powerful impact on the body. Many of the aches, pains, illnesses, and diseases you encounter in your body stem from the way you relate to it. In a very direct manner, if you don't pay attention to your body's needs, you may engage in self-destructive behaviours, such as excessive alcohol consumption, drug use, lack of exercise, and compulsive eating habits. These can all lead to putting your health at risk.

Beyond the positive physical impacts of loving-kindness, how you mentally relate to your body also has impacts—however indirectly—that can impact your quality of life. The western medical profession acknowledges that stress is one of the leading causes of illnesses. Those predisposed to certain illnesses are at a greater likelihood of experiencing the detrimental effects of that illness if they are chronically stressed.

When you do inevitably become ill, as you will at some point in your life, the way you relate to the physical symptoms of that illness will greatly affect your sense of well-being and happiness. If you can relate to your body in a manner that is accepting, even the most horrific aches and pains might not seem so bad. There are examples of meditators who, diagnosed with terminal cancer, make peace with their body and die later than expected, after having continued to live a happy life. The human body is naturally inclined toward a state of balance.

Our auto-regulatory mechanisms attempt to regulate body temperature to a comfortable norm, for example through sweating to expel heat or shivering to create motion and warmth. Our liver and intestines attempt to expel toxins from the body, and our cardiovascular system works hard to ensure all regions of the body are adequately supplied with nutrients. Many of the illnesses we experience stem from us relating to the body with tension, control, tightness, and stress, which in turn disrupts these mechanisms. The ability to accept the body as it is, regardless of what we're experiencing, is equivalent to leaving the body alone and letting it do what it intuitively knows how to do. Even in cases where death is imminent, accepting this process allows us to die more peacefully, rather than in a state of stress or anxiety.

A practical way that you can develop this state of open acceptance of your body is to meditate with the mantra "I am safe. I am OK." Breath in, "I am safe" and out, "I am OK." As you repeat this, observe the physical sensations of pain or discomfort that arise. Notice how the quality of awareness and kindness is separate from the pain. Even in the midst of pain, that awareness is not the pain itself. There is a state of purity in that awareness that can be accepting of the experience, whether pleasant, unpleasant, or neutral. The more you practise residing with the feeling of being safe and well in that awareness, the more comforting that space feels. During painful times, that space can feel like the eye of a hurricane. That calm, comforting awareness is what allows you to be at ease with the torrential downpour, being within it yet remaining dry.

If you have problem areas in your body, you may want to actively direct loving-kindness toward that area. Similar to other techniques, you must first spend time settling into your present-moment awareness. When relatively settled, and having conjured the energy of loving-kindness, begin to direct this energy into your body. Start from the centre of your chest, where your breath is most coarse and physically evident, and focus on breathing into your chest through the pores of your skin, rather than through your nose. Imagine the pores of your skin being able to absorb oxygen and expel carbon dioxide, and with each inhale, picture the breath flowing in through your skin into your chest, and flowing out with the exhale. As you draw oxygen in and out through the pores of your skin, imagine health, energy, happiness, well-being—or any other word which has a positive meaning to you—flowing in with the inhale, and release any tension, stress, or negativity with the exhale.

Gradually, you can progress to other parts of your body. You can move upward to the throat, pulling air into your throat through the pores of your skin, inhaling positive healing energy. Then proceed to breathe negativity out through your skin. You can progress down to your abdomen, doing the same, and eventually outward to the extremities of your body. You may notice that certain areas are more painful or that you're holding stress or tension in certain parts of your body, such as the shoulders and neck, or sadness and anxiety in your abdomen. Though it may feel uncomfortable, spend more time breathing positivity into these particular parts of your body.

Caring for your body in this very attuned and sensitive manner may make aches and illnesses lessen or disappear. Some meditators have experienced the unexplained and unexpected when they suddenly notice that the chronic back pain they've been living with for decades disappears as a result of meditation, or they may feel a sense of ease and relief when anxiety that has been building up in their body suddenly vanishes.

CHAPTER 9

Necessary Ingredients and Red Flags

"Be here now. Be someplace later. Is that so complicated?"

– DAVID M. BADER

As you continue your loving-kindness practice, you may notice times when your practice thrives and other times when it falls apart. When it is thriving, take the time to notice and reflect on what conditions are present. What causes things to fall apart? By reflecting, you are developing your own wisdom and becoming your own guide and teacher.

There are three key elements essential to a strong loving-kindness practice:

Ease, Gentleness and Consistency

It's worth repeating that you shouldn't force the love; let it come at its own pace. You might sometimes sit and immediately feel the sensation of love and kindness. At other times it may feel like it takes an eternity. More important than the quickness of the mind to evoke this emotion is the consistency in which you practise. The more you do it, the stronger your mind will grow and the easier it will be to access that feeling of loving-kindness. Like with any habit, consistency strengthens the neural pathways in your brain, making that emotion habitual. As these pathways strengthen, you will find many of the neurotic and controlling tendencies of your mind weaken in favour of what is a more peaceful and gentle way of living.

Employing Wisdom

Knowing when to invoke effort and when to invoke ease are both important. Invoking ease of loving-kindness is necessary if your heart is heavy or still. However, if your mind is light and free, you may wish to progress to a more advanced stage of meditation. In either case, you should be reviewing your successes to determine what went right. What is conducive to joy and peace, and what isn't?

In Thailand, they often say that the meditator should watch their mind the way a mother protects her child. The mother allows the child to take a few steps, but still keeps an eye on the child. If the child is walking fine with no issue, the mother does not intervene, but simply observes, lovingly and kindly. If the mother notices the child is about to fall, or pick up something harmful, the mother immediately swoops in to stop the child. Once the child is stable again, or the object is relinquished, the mother allows the child to walk again, continuing to observe.

Be watchful, aware, ardent, not lax in observing your mind. Be kind and gentle, offering correction to your mind when needed, but not in a forceful, harsh, or angry way. Watch your mind closely with love and compassion.

Unbounded

Develop a perception of loving-kindness that is without limit—unbounded—and that is not only directed to those close to you or those who are easy to love. While it can be difficult to initially extend loving-kindness toward difficult people, you should eventually work toward that. This does not mean creating an idealized sort of love, then shaming yourself when you act in ways that are inconsistent with that ideal. It means testing the bounds of your mind, to see that you can dislike someone deeply and yet still feel acceptance, love, and kindness. This includes yourself, the most difficult person to love.

This comprehensive set of instructions should get you started in the practice of loving-kindness. Feel free to return to this section again and again as you practise; you may find new insights that become relevant or new techniques you wish to try. Importantly, do not forget that no matter what you think, you are capable of giving yourself all the loving-kindness you need. Your loving-kindness is capable of changing your world.

Part Three
Beyond You and Others

CHAPTER 10

Climate Change

"Climate change is no longer some far-off problem; it is happening here; it is happening now."

— BARACK OBAMA

Perhaps one of the most pressing global issues of our modern society is that of global climate change. The scientific consensus on the detrimental consequences of global climate change has reached an undeniable tipping point, with the evidence stacked high. As individuals battling against the many pressures of daily life, we are frequently made to feel disempowered to take action on larger issues, such as climate change. Caring about such an important issue can be emotionally overwhelming.

We try to recycle, take public transit, and be more conscious about our dietary habits, only to turn on the television and see mass deaths and illness from a global pandemic, stifling air pollution in India and China, species on the verge of extinction, and climate catastrophes decimating vulnerable populations, let alone the myriad of other issues we're trying to cope with, such as the prospect of war. Eventually, we become cynical and feel the world is doomed regardless and resign ourselves to the sentiment that we have no ability to create any form of lasting impact.

In these trying times, I want to advocate for something quite radical. I want to advocate for a different form of climate change. The earth and its inhabitants are impacted by the climate, and the climate, too, is shaped by the actions of earth's inhabitants in a reciprocal relationship. Similarly, we are influenced by the climate of our own lives. It's time to take control of climate change in our own lives.

The story that follows demonstrates how we change and adapt with the environment.

The Parrot Twins

Long ago, two parrot twins were born into a loving parrot family. Their parents, being the kind and generous parrots they were, wanted nothing more than to give their newborn twins the best possible shot at survival and one day have parrot families of their own. After much deliberation, the parents decided it was best to fly south to a forest with less competition for territory, and plenty of delicious nuts, seeds and insects for sustenance. After a few months of preparation teaching the young parrot twins to fly, the parents felt ready for the big move. After a good night's sleep, the parrot family departed at dawn.

They flew for hours, over winding rivers and dense jungle thicket, across open plains and sun-kissed mountain peaks. The journey was spectacularly stunning. However, they had just passed the halfway point when things took a turn for the worse. An unpredictable storm was rapidly approaching from the west. The mother parrot was the first to spot the storm, and squawked for the family to speed things up. Flap as they might, the storm was suddenly upon them. Violent rain and winds pulled and pushed the parrots left and right, up and down, despite their best efforts. Fear quickly increased, as the parrot twins squawked pleadingly for their parents. The father parrot attempted to turn back with the young parrot twins, but was losing sight of the twins, as their smaller wings wouldn't allow them to keep up with the parents. With a sudden roaring crack of thunder, a bolt of lightning lit the sky, nearly hitting the parrot family, and a blustery wind pulled the parrot twins into a downward spiral. Their parents desperately grasped for them, but in a matter of seconds the parrot twins were out of sight, lost in the deadly storm.

Falling rapidly, the twins were separated, lost sight of each other and crash landed into separate areas of the jungle below. The first parrot landed in a particularly dense thicket that happened to be inhabited by aggressive and hardened wildlife poachers who revelled in the thrill of hunting and killing anything they could get their hands on. The second parrot was more fortunate, landing in a beautiful stretch of open soft grass. This particular patch of grass was home to several smaller wooden huts where friendly hermits maintained a wildlife sanctuary for injured animals.

The first parrot barely had a chance to recover consciousness, before he was violently snatched up by the wildlife poachers. Conveniently, the poachers had a need for entertainment, and decided they would cage the parrot, prodding and poking him to make him dance. The second parrot on the other hand, was much more fortunate. The concerned and kind hermits who noticed his crash landing rushed over to ensure he was still alive. Taking him in, they nursed him back to good health, and ensured he had wide open space to practise flying while his wings recovered.

Over time, the first parrot, being a parrot, learned to emulate the particularly foul language of the poachers. Whenever another animal would walk by, the parrot would curse like a sailor! I'll save your eyes from having to read the words this parrot used. Similarly, the second parrot also emulated the words of his kind captors. Whenever any of the hermits would walk by, the parrot would kindly compliment them, using only positive and supportive phrases.

A few years passed until one day a change of circumstance occurred. The captors of the first parrot woke to sirens and the sound of fast approaching vehicles. Law enforcement had tracked down these mercenary poachers and before long, several of them were fleeing, with the rest in handcuffs. In all the commotion, the first parrot's cage was knocked over and he was able to flee. Not sure where to go, he recalled his parents and the journey that had separated them, and headed in the direction that he assumed had been their original destination. The second parrot, on the other hand, was quite comfortable where he was. His hosts were gracious and generous, and he was receiving more than enough food. In fact he had grown quite plump! However, something was missing. The second parrot longed for home, and wished to return to his family. He decided to leave his hosts, thanking them for their kindness, gathering his possessions and flying south.

After grieving the loss of their children for several years, imagine the parents' surprise when their two parrot twins appeared at the branches of their home. The parents, beaming ear to ear, embraced their two parrot twins. However, it quickly became apparent that something was just not right. Their first parrot son scowled and pushed them off, his ruffled feathers barely concealing a look of anger. In contrast, the second parrot remarked on how happy he was to see his long-lost parents, crying tears of joy and quickly filling them in on the lovely hermits he had resided with.

Soon, this stark contrast was too much for the parents to bear, and they inquired as to why these two twins, who were inseparable at birth, were so different. The first parrot described how his patch of forest was inhabited by cruel poachers. They fought with one another, stole, wouldn't help each other, spoke harmful and harsh words, told lies, traded in deceit, and stole anything in sight. In contrast the second parrot described being so fortunate to fall into a forest where sages were living. Everyday, he would meditate with the wise hermits, perform communal chores together, compliment *each other with kindness, and support one another. Their speech, actions and intentions were kind. The parents quickly concluded that both parrots had become a product of their environment.*

This story mirrors the findings of behavioural psychologists in the past and the present, their theories explaining how people and animals change and adapt according to their environment. Just as the first parrot became harsh, the second parrot became kind due to the environment and where he was raised. Such is the power of our environment and the people we are surrounded with.

Taking Control of Climate Change

Now is the time to take control of our own lives, to take control of climate change. In other words, it's time to actively put into place the circumstances that are conducive to our own well-being and happiness. Though much of the larger socio-political climate can be out of our control, the climate of our own lives is strongly influenced by our perceptions, thoughts, speech, actions, and the behaviour of those we surround ourselves with.

In any environment, those who are happy, healthy, kind, compassionate, and generous act like a form of magnet, pulling people toward them with their joy and love for life. Being surrounded by that type of person, it's hard not to have their infectious laughter or compassionate gaze warm your heart and make you feel safe. As we go through life, we are like atoms colliding, leaving each other changed by our interactions. We can witness this type of conditioning in families: Children who are treated kindly—with love and support—tend to grow up to be happy, healthy individuals. In contrast, those who sadly have to face emotional and physical abuse, neglect, or lack of access to basic resources, have significant hurdles to overcome. They are more likely to become dysfunctional adults, perpetuating the same injustices toward their own children in a vicious cycle of anger and unhappiness.

We need not look any further than our own dark Canadian history to witness the lasting, intergenerational impacts that a negative climate can have on a human being. Examining the history of colonialism in Canada, we see how a climate of hate, fear, violence, and prejudice was created. White settlers seized Indigenous land for resource extraction and used manipulative and inhumane tactics—such as forced starvation and physical segregation—to create a situation of dependence, displacing many thousands of Indigenous peoples from their lands, breaking treaty agreements, and destroying families and cultures in the process. This genocide has created long-lasting impacts, with Indigenous youth still experiencing the intergenerational trauma of residential schools, as well as the effects of a Canadian culture that still harbours deep-seated racism toward Indigenous peoples.

In stark contrast, one of my close disciples had the privilege of sitting on interfaith community councils and participating in activities with multifaith communities. Being a visible minority with a racialized last name, he described his moving experience of entering into spaces of faith that were not his own, expecting to be faced with suspicious resistance, or possibly even overt racism, only to be warmly welcomed with open arms. Rather than being pushed to convert or change his views, he was accepted into community dinners, events, and gatherings simply by virtue of the fact that he was another human being willing to step into that space with an open mind. The degree of kindness and acceptance moved him to tears. These were climates of love and support, irrespective of creed, class, or religion. This is not to suggest that all communities are like this, but to show the power that a positive climate can have on one's sense of emotional well-being and support.

In our lives, we may not always have a choice over what cards we were dealt. However, we all have a choice as to what type of climate we wish to curate. We can harbour fear, anger, jealousy, hatred, and mistrust, creating a climate of darkness that consumes our hearts. We can become the settlers and oppressors of others in our own lives, and of ourselves, thereby destroying our own happiness and making the world feel like a cruel and cold place. Or, we can choose to be those with faith in the power of kindfulness, suspending our conditioned biases and accepting and nurturing the ups and downs that life brings our way, with open arms. The choice to take control of climate change is ours, and ours alone.

CHAPTER 11

Shifting Perspectives

"If you change the way you look at things, the things you look at change."

— WAYNE DYER

Though I emphasize that you must make a conscious shift in your perspective about your impact on climate, I won't trivialize the amount of effort necessary. Without mindfulness and wisdom, it's easy to miss or underestimate how much you are influenced by your environment and how rapidly you get caught up in habitual ways of reacting to your experiences. You can quickly lose control over your actions and consequently, your life. You can easily get trapped in a cycle of uncontrolled cause and effect.

Before the pandemic, I was fortunate to return to Bangladesh for a few weeks. I was engaged in various activities to help support local communities, including handing out care packages and monetary donations to individuals living on the street.

Closer to the end of my trip, I was able to spend a few days reconnecting with my sister. One day, when I returned from giving talks and handing out care packages, my sister said that I didn't look like myself, that I looked off. When I caught a glimpse of my reflection, I immediately realized what it was.

My usual warm smile had been replaced by flat, narrow lips; my glowing cheeks were sunken and sullen; and my eyelids looked like someone had strapped weights to them. I felt OK on the surface, but in reality, the lack of relaxation was showing on my face. I became aware that my perspective had shifted after spending so much time speaking with homeless people and hearing countless stories of pain, struggles and suffering.

At some point during the day, I had allowed myself to operate on autopilot, and in the process, I lost my mindfulness and awareness. My perception became skewed by the negative stories, and I was no longer able to see a positive side. Once I made a point of redirecting my attention, I could recall the joy of people feeling that they had been heard and the bonds that had been formed from sharing difficulties. I could remember warm smiles and tears of joy when I handed money and material goods to people who would almost never receive a second glance from passersby. Recalling these things immediately brought joy to my heart, and my complexion changed almost instantly. The next day, when I went out, I could feel the joy spreading to those around me.

My personal experience demonstrates how the mind can quickly be influenced by the environment if we lack mindful awareness. This experience also shows how mindful awareness, together with an intentional shift—redirection—allows us to see the beauty in others as well as in a situation.

To shift your perspective, use the following three steps:

Step 1: Become Aware

This first step in shifting perspective is to become aware of your current state of mind. Take a moment to check in with yourself. Ask yourself ask how your mind and body are feeling right at that moment. You may find that your neck is tight because you've been carrying around the tension of a stressful day, or you may have a knot in your stomach, chest, or throat because of a particularly difficult conversation you had. You may discover that the mind is currently light and joyous or anxious and dispersed by thoughts that arise in the course of a typical day. Or, like I felt in Bangladesh, you may notice a persistent mood, such as feeling emotionally flat. Taking stock of your current state of mind is an important step. Without this important first step, you won't know what needs to change. If you're not aware, you are on autopilot. Would you want your surgeon to perform heart surgery without having actually diagnosed you?

Step 2: Investigate

Once you've become aware of how your mind and body feel, patiently and persistently investigate the main causes of the progression of your emotions and their relation to both internal and external stimuli.

You may overthink or analyze your thoughts and feelings and judge them. You may call uncomfortable feelings—such as frustration and anger—bad and feel that you need to do something about them. You may develop complex judgments around the way you are feeling, feeling guilty about your changing mental state or feeling inadequate.

Rather than become obsessively self-critical and analytical, shift your investigating technique to patient reflection. You should attempt to patiently be with those feelings, irrespective of what they are and how uncomfortable they may be. When you persist patiently, you will notice a certain pattern. Many of the feelings you developed from past experiences to protect you are now unhelpful. For example, you may have been neglected as a child and, to cope, formed a sense of independence around dealing with emotions on your own. You may have rejected the support of others because you thought you couldn't count on them. This may have been helpful in insulating you from suffering in the moment, but it led to imbalances. You had trouble opening up to others and became less accepting of your own emotional vulnerability, which resulted in to isolation and loneliness.

By investigating yourself in this way, you will begin to get to the core of the patterns that plague you and cause you to repeat the same self-destructive tendencies. By simply investigating your patterns of anger or frustration, for example, you can begin to question your own thoughts, rather than simply believing whatever you think to be true. This allows you to open up to your current state—both good and bad—with wholesome acceptance. From a place of acceptance, you are then equipped to take the action needed to redirect.

Step 3: Redirect

The third and final step in this process of shifting perspective is to redirect. Like a familiar hiking trail, your mental habits can tread the same old pathways. You can lament for months, or even years, over that person who wronged you or the partner who broke your heart. You can repeatedly torture yourself with thoughts about the terrible thing someone said about you or find that you're getting into relationships with the same types of people, which all end up deteriorating in the same way.

Seeing your way out of these tenacious patterns requires putting forth patient, gentle, and persistent effort toward redirecting your thoughts. First, it is important that you be fully aware of your patterns and their attributes. It is a mistake to skip Step One: Become aware and Step Two: Investigate and head straight to redirect. This can be a tactic of avoidance. Because you may begin to feel discomfort around your feelings of loneliness, for example, you may too quickly clutch at your phone or turn to Netflix to see what's trending. Or you may be in an uncomfortable conversation with someone who holds different views and immediately look for a way out or a reason to blame them and react in anger. In more extreme situations, you may develop addictions to things like alcohol, drugs, or pornography as a means of redirecting your mind from the painful emotional and physical sensations you experience through your memories and your old habits.

Consequently, it is very important that you first utilize the steps—become aware and investigate—to understand your old tendencies and their root causes. Often, this intentional action of lifting the veil on your fears, worries, doubts, and anxieties allows you to penetrate to the core and see the causes. In most instances, you have developed repetitive patterns to feel safe and secure. At some point in your life, this default coping mechanism may have served the purpose of protecting you from greater emotional and psychological harm, but it is now outdated and causing you grief.

Seeing the roots of your emotional difficulties can reduce or shut down your distress. Your mind will then begin to feel at ease with your current situation. In other situations, redirection might require you to take concrete action, such as standing up for injustices even though your conditioning might make you to want shut down emotionally. Or the action may be to remain silent when you would have ordinarily exploded in anger, or you made decide to remove yourself from relationships and circumstances that would be distractions from your peace and well-being.

In all circumstances, this innate ability of your mind to redirect itself toward your peace in the present moment and take action from a place of kind awareness is always there, but it requires that you possess a willingness to look at how you're really feeling right now. This takes courage and diligent persistence, but it can be done.

Paying It Forward

You weren't born with an impure mind or heart, but you do become the product of conditioning. You need only look at a smiling baby to see that you are born innocent and pure. Though you may be born with certain tendencies as a result of genetic predispositions, at your core, you possess the capacity to adapt. However, just as you can become the product of your environment, you can also become an influencer in your environment. You can contribute to creating a climate of love, acceptance, and well-being through your actions and reactions. Similarly, you can contribute to creating a climate of anger, dishonesty, and fear.

As you engage in the process of becoming aware, investigating, and redirecting, you will begin to notice the many positive traits that you may not be aware you innately possess. These abilities include resilience, adaptability, self-compassion, and equanimity. Resilience in your ability to be with negative emotions without judging them or trying to push them away. Adaptability in responding to ever-changing situations with grace. Self-compassion in how you connect to your own struggle using kindness. Equanimity in your ability to move through life with ease and acceptance despite difficulties.

Just as you think about the climate you wish to create in yourself, you should think about what climate you wish to create for the people interacting with you. A simple way to start doing this is to reflect on one relationship, person, situation, or experience that is meaningful to you. What makes it so important? How can you recreate that for others?

For me, I feel inspired when I come into a meditation hall and see people from all walks of life and of all ages peacefully awaiting meditation in silence. What makes that so inspiring is that everyone is there for a collective purpose. There is a certain degree of mutual acceptance present in the room. There is also a sense of ease knowing that no one will be judged or ridiculed for their presence. Reflecting on this experience, I recognize that acceptance is an important element in a positive climate. As such, I endeavour to approach every interaction, irrespective of who the person is, with non-judgmental acceptance.

Now, imagine if everyone picked just one theme such as this and began bringing that element to every new environment they entered into. You live in a symbiotic relationship with your climate. Your immediate environment influences you, and you, too, can influence it. Reflecting using awareness, investigation, and redirection can allow you to cut through conditioning and replace negative mental patterns with wholesome healthy ones. You can bring healthy changes to your surroundings to help spread that change and create the climate that not only you wish to live in, but one that other people wish to live in as well.

CHAPTER 12

The Happiness Pill

"The greatest disease in the West today is not TB or leprosy; it is being unwanted, unloved, and uncared for."

MOTHER TERESA

We are on the cusp of change as global movements bring the atrocities committed against large populations to our awareness; the effects of climate change become a lived reality threatening safety and well-being; and political unrest, violence, and instability seem more widespread. The global pandemic led to some heightened fears, mass closures, the suspension of services, widespread deaths, mistrust in government, denial of science, and heightened extremism. Furthermore, levels of poverty, homelessness, domestic violence, and substance abuse have increased at frighteningly high levels and show no signs of decreasing.

For many of us, these changes outside of our control can cause us to react in ways we typically would not, leading to a decline in mental health and well-being. In many western countries, there has been a spike in the use of antidepressants, with doctors in England giving out over seventy million prescriptions in 2018 alone and this even before the pandemic. Now, more than ever, the increase in drug and alcohol abuse, along with the decline in mental health, is felt throughout the world, with the US hitting the deadliest year of substance abuse in 2020. In my practice as a Buddhist monk and spiritual advisor, I regularly assist people who are struggling with their mental health. While the causes and conditions vary, the common theme is that people are looking for a way out of their suffering, a way to be truly at peace and know inner happiness.

There are countless recommendations a doctor might give to improve your physical health, including a healthy diet, exercise, and taking in the outdoors. And if you're unwell, you also might be prescribed medication.

But what about mental health? For those of us who may not be clinically depressed and require medication or therapy, is there a "happiness pill" we can take to feel happy? There is. The Happiness Pill is a combination of equal parts good deeds, speech, and thoughts left to ferment through meditation and warmed at an appropriate temperature using smiles, laughter, and care. This means that you should speak in a gentle and kind way and say things that uplift others. Do things that will benefit you and those around you, such as giving generously when the opportunity arises, and avoid work and actions that might cause loss of life or physical or psychological harm. You must also remember not to harm yourself by overextending yourself. You should nurture the positive thoughts that arise in your mind and avoid investing mental energy in thoughts of self-blame, anger, and stress. And, importantly, you should ferment this combination through a meditative practice of at least fifteen minutes per day as a way of checking how your mind is affected. A meditative practice will also help you develop the mindfulness and awareness to notice when you're not adequately applying all of the components, as you won't be effective if even one of these is missing.

Finally, you should remember to laugh and smile at all the good, ridiculous, annoying, frustrating, and exciting moments and everything in between. As you smile more, others will also smile more. When you speak in a kind and gentle manner, people will feel comfortable around you and enjoy conversing with you. Just as you want to be safe and happy in your own way, everyone else also wants to be safe and happy. By refraining from harming others and performing only good deeds you signal to others that they can be safe, free, and emotionally open in your company. You will feel more love and acceptance when you see that people are able to be themselves around you. When you meditate, you are able to recharge and rest your mind. In this way, you can freely continue to be a source of joy for others without feeling drained, exhausted, or harming yourself.

You'll also be happy to know there are no contraindications to the Happiness Pill. Pregnant? Your baby just might be born smiling too. Currently on medication? No problem, keep following your doctor's advice. The Happiness Pill formula has the lovely side effect of helping with ailments that you might have.

There are five steps to the Happiness Pill:

Step 1: Prevent

If you've ever gone hiking in the remote wilderness, you have likely seen warning signs about the presence of black bears. These native animals, although cute and cuddly at first glance, can be extremely territorial and, as a result, potentially deadly. If you take your safety and well-being seriously, you'll be on guard in bear territory. Perhaps you'll come equipped with bear spray and a warning bell and learn the appropriate methods to scare them off.

These warning signs act as a means of prevention. They are there to ensure that you don't engage in conduct that might be harmful to you, the nature around you, or any of the other hikers. These types of signs exist everywhere, from "Mind the

Gap" signs at subway stations to "Don't Text and Drive" and "Fasten Your Seat Belt" signs on highways and airplanes.

These types of signs also exist in your mind, to warn you not to cause harm. If you believe in caring for your mental health as much as your physical well-being, it's important for you to learn to recognize when these signs arise and prevent actions that lead you to harm yourself or others. Feeling angry or frustrated with someone is a warning sign. The feeling of tension in your chest, your face burning as blood rushes in your cheeks, and your vision blurring are all warning signs that are telling you to stop what you are doing and calm yourself before acting—or reacting—otherwise you may harm yourself or others. The physical signs you manifest are trying to keep you on a safe path.

These warning signs can also be hidden in positive emotions. Not heeding the warning signs hidden in positive emotions can become unhealthy. Cravings, longings, and substance abuse are all examples of warning signs disguised as pleasure. You may not understand this during the peak of the effects, but you will be able to when you reach the low of the consequences.

At the low point, you will experience the harm first-hand. In this situation, your body gives two warning signs. The first is the mind-numbing sensation of pleasure that came with the peak, and the second is the equally mind-numbing sensation of hollowness and pain that happens after the peak. The momentary pleasure followed by the anxiety of having been unfaithful or the fear and guilt felt after inflicting harm on another living being . . . these are all warning signs.

Once you pay attention to these signs—and commit to not engaging in harmful behaviour or refrain from them in the future—you are practising prevention. You're preventing unwholesome habits from developing in the mind, which would cause future unhappiness. You are also stopping yourself from forming cravings and addictions. By preventing these habits from arising, and gaining control over your life, you are safe-guarding your current state of well-being and happiness.

Step 2: Eliminate

If you're a typical human being, you're likely to know that you have a tendency to ignore some warning signs. This is where elimination comes in. First, try not to repeat actions . . . especially the harmful ones. If you notice yourself losing mindfulness, you shouldn't judge yourself for doing so. Rather, when you do have periods with more mental clarity, investigate why you took the wrong path in the first place. When you recognize the origin of these tendencies, try to see what you can do to reduce them. When you realize that you are engaging in these tendencies, such as speaking harshly or deceiving or harming others, work on finding methods to remove them. One of the most powerful ways is to return to a kindfulness practice. By practising kindful-ness toward yourself and others, you can prevent going down the same old paths and help heal many of the wounds that cause you to make bad choices in the first place.

Step 3: Cultivate

You may want to get rid of unwanted negative tendencies, but you may not know how to. In the previous step, elimination, we talked about identifying what contributed to negative ten-dencies. In this cultivation step, identify all the times that you didn't act with your usual tendencies. Pay particular attention to the good things you've done and the effect and emotions that the good actions produced in your mind and in your body. Also think about generous and kind acts others have done, and notice how those actions affected you and the emotions that arose. Try to replicate those kind acts for other people.

Try to engage in appropriate thoughts, speech, and behaviour to yield the desired result of producing happiness. Smile and be kind more often, even to your pains and sorrows. The warmth of your kindness to yourself and others will radiate outward and help burn out any overgrowth of pain or negativity.

This also means developing positive physical and mental behaviours. On the physical side, exercising regularly, consuming healthy foods, and avoiding the consumption of intoxicants are very positive. These help in supporting and cultivating positive mental behaviours as well. On the mental side, engaging in a daily practice of meditation for even as little as fifteen to twenty minutes will help build a visible positive momentum in your life. It will help when making difficult decisions or calming yourself and will lead to an overall increased sense of personal well-being. More importantly, it will give you the ability to see where, when, and why negative mental patterns arise and when and why they cease.

Step 4: Preserve and Maintain

In this step, take the time to notice the good traits that you already have, as well as the new good traits that you are beginning to develop. If you're having difficulty doing this, take a piece of paper and draw a line down the middle, then label the left-hand side, "The Things That Are Good about Me" and label the right side, "The Things I Don't Like about Myself." Sit, and give the list some serious thought. You may only come up with a few things for the left side and many for the right side. Add the small acts of kindness you did to your list, as even these could have made someone's day. Perhaps you opened a door for someone recently. Maybe you listened to someone else's problems, helped someone who dropped something, or even just showed patience when someone else was particularly frustrating. Add all these to the left side of your list.

When you've finally finished your list, you might find that the left-hand side of your list is much longer than the right. Don't worry if it is not, as this next step is the most crucial. Tear off the right-hand side of the paper you titled "The Things I Don't Like about Myself," crumple it up, and throw it away.

The rest of the paper, "The Things That Are Good about Me," that lists all your good traits and actions will now become your reference points for preservation and maintenance. Continue to repeat these good actions and nurture these traits. Try developing new and different good actions that you may have experienced from someone else. Use your mindfulness practice to notice when you act in a manner that is in line with these traits.

Step 5: Recollect the Practice

Suppose your doctor gave you a prescription, you took the time and trouble to have the prescription filled at the pharmacy, and then you got home and locked the pill bottle away in the medicine cabinet and forgot about it. The entire process of going to the doctor served little purpose, and the medicine is useless since you will not take it.

Similarly, it's important to remember the previous four steps and continually make an effort to maintain and develop them. It is what allows happiness to grow. No matter where you go, if you can maintain these qualities, you'll be where you need to be.

The Happiness Pill summarizes how you can go about reorienting the way you relate to the world around you. Though there is no actual happiness pill, engaging in a practice of inner reflection can act as your Happiness Pill. Preparing your mind for this type of development requires preventing unwholesome thoughts, speech, and actions; eliminating existing ones; cultivating your existing positive states of mind; maintaining your positive states; and recollecting and repeating the practice.

CHAPTER 13

The Kindful Tree

"Do you want to know who you are? Don't ask. Act! Action will delineate and define you."

THOMAS JEFFERSON

In this chapter, we will expand on the practice of kindfulness. Using the Kindful Tree, we will demonstrate how you can create the change you wish to see in yourself and in the world around you. Recall that the tree is supported by three roots:

- The roots of wisdom, comprising of kind perspective and kind intention
- The roots of relationships, comprising of kind speech, kind action, and kind livelihood
- The roots of awareness, comprising of kind effort, kind mindfulness, and kind stillness

Together these three sets of roots flow and interconnect, interrelate and support one another to nurture and grow the Kindful Tree.

The Roots of Wisdom:
Kind Perspective and Kind Intention

Kind Perspective is based on an understanding of cause and effect. It involves understanding the importance of your mental world, your physical world, and the way the two interrelate. In other words, kind perspective is the willingness to investigate the impact your thoughts, speech, and actions have on your well-being and the well-being of others. It also asks that you not only explore cause and effect from the perspective of your own internal world, but also as it relates to others.

Importantly, kind perspective is exploring the view that you have a responsibility to ensure your own happiness. If you don't explore this view, you won't be motivated to examine your patterns of thought, speech, and actions because you believe your happiness is entirely external to you. The consequence will be to consistently seek happiness through gratification of your senses, never finding inner stability or peace. Furthermore, it will cause you to feel bitter and jealous when you witness others being happy. I say this to emphasize that kind perspective implies the willingness to explore and challenge your own views.

Reflect on what kind of person you would like to be in the future. Ideally, this type of reflection needs to be planted at a young age and consistently nurtured so that it can grow and develop. When we discuss education, its importance, and reform, we tend to overemphasize the significance of individual achievements. We prioritize "A's" and high GPAs over happiness. Even when we become adults, we idolize the ultra-rich and celebrities for their success and wealth. However, this type of intellectual education or wealth and success alone do not guarantee a kindful life for that person. This is not to say that intellectual education should not be valued, but education must also include developing emotional intelligence. Children should witness and engage in kind heartedness. For instance, in Japan, before parents send their children to school, they provide home schooling on Japanese culture and values. This includes teaching children how to show respect to others. Children learn that a particular action could hurt others, and hurting others can hurt you. The child learns how to act in ways that do not harm people. They also learn to be more mindful and cautious before acting. Kind perspective is about being able to know and feel the impact of your actions on your emotional world and that of others. Kind perspective is the process of developing emotional intelligence about yourself and about other living beings.

Harvard researcher Daniel Goleman remarks that emotional intelligence is what distinguishes some of the world's most successful leaders. This is characterized by traits such as self-awareness, emotional regulation, social awareness, and relationship management. Another way of looking at kind perspective is to view it as the expansion of your awareness. Learn to perceive and understand the emotive cause-and-effect relationship and the role you play in this relationship, so that it remains stable.

Kind perspective is also exploring the impact of your good actions, that whatever you say or do has an impact. Whether you throw kindness or unkindness into the universe, it will be returned to you. Some people might argue that there are plenty of rich or powerful people who do terrible things and get away with it. Viewed in a fixed moment in time, it can indeed appear that way. However, at some point, those individuals will experience their own suffering resulting from their action, whether it's in the form or developing substance addictions, alienating their loved ones, or going to jail. If one delves in deeper, those who seem externally happy using exploitation and greed are in fact miserable, as they constantly fear losing their power and attempt to control the entire world around them.

The point is not to look to others and hope they suffer as a result of their bad deeds, but to look to your own mind and see how you are benefiting or suffering as a result of your mental state, thoughts, intentions, actions, and speech. Kind perspective entails recognizing that when you harm others, that harm comes back to haunt you psychologically. You carry guilt or anger and repeatedly end up in situations where you react in the same manner. You become unable to recognize why you aren't happy and constantly blame your unhappiness on others or on the world around you. Kind perspective is the willingness to take charge of your own happiness by recognizing this ripple effect.

I share the following story to illustrate that even I can have family conflict, but it doesn't have to rule my happiness. During the COVID-19 pandemic, I began distributing essential items to people in need. My brother was upset that I was giving items to others rather than to him and his family, even though I had helped them out as well. Despite his criticism, I continued to give to others, with faith that my good deeds would come back to me. Many people expressed how inspired they felt by these actions and reached out to offer additional resources. My decision to persist with kindness—guided by wisdom—in the face of my brother's criticism ultimately led to greater benefit. Whereas my brother suffered from anger due to his greed, my mind rejoiced due to my good deeds.

You need to trust in your good actions. Just because one person criticizes you doesn't mean you should hold on to that criticism. You need to have faith that even if one person doesn't return kindness, the universe will return it because the universe witnesses what you do. Consider where your universe lives and is experienced in the confines of your mind. Just as you cannot hide your unwholesome actions forever, you cannot hide from the benefits of your kind actions. One way or another, each catches up to you because you carry the whole weight of your actions in your mind.

Finally, kindful perspective means appreciating where you currently stand. This means taking the time to do an honest appraisal of what you currently have in your life. This means bravely acknowledging interdependence, having gratitude for the good, and recognizing where problems exist in your life.

Kind intention is setting the goal to explore what peace of mind entails in this very moment. It means a willingness to explore what the causes of your problems are and how best to address them. It is not just about exploring the external causes but the internal ones as well. How are you relating to the external and internal world? Are you associating to it in a way that creates problems? Though you may not have answers at this stage, are you curious enough to ask the questions?

Kind intention is setting the goal of acting in a way that produces positive benefits for yourself and for others. More specifically, it is the intention to speak and act in a way that is free of greed, hatred, delusion, or ill will, not out of blind faith, but out of an appreciation of the cause-and-effect relationship you are exploring with kind perspective.

It is also a shifting of attention away from violence, harming, or slandering and a shift toward peace, acceptance, love, and compassion. Even if you only make it this far in tracing the Kindful Tree, you have already shifted your internal world, such that you are happy in the world of your mind.

Finally, it's important to mention that kind intention is fluid, as it is fed by the other roots. As you explore your relationship with others, you may speak or act in ways that create harm despite what you believe at the time to be well intentioned. You must be willing to regularly revisit your intentions to determine if they are truly kindful. Do they have positive benefits for you and others? Conversely, you may step outside of your comfort zone and give to someone or say supportive words to someone who has wronged you, which at the time might seem scary or evoke resistance in you. Does this have a positive benefit? If so, what intention was behind that action? Was it kindful, and if so, how can you nurture that? As you trace the roots of the Kindful Tree, continue to notice how each of the roots interrelate to support the other. Read how the young king in the following story uses the roots of wisdom to help improve his subjects' happiness.

The Kindful Kingdom

There once was a kindful young king, who loved giving to people in need and was compassionate to everyone. Yet, he noticed that not all of his subjects were happy, which puzzled him. Thus, he began searching for a method to ensure that everyone in his realm was happy. Every so often, he would disguise himself and stroll through the kingdom without attracting any attention. He would observe and experience the lifestyle of his subjects. One day he would live among the homeless and experience their pain and hear their struggles to survive. Another day he would live among the farmers and discern their difficulties, listening to conversations about failure of the crops or the cruelty of the landowners. He would travel at night, to catch a glimpse of the challenges women and children faced trying to find safety once the sun went down. He would listen in on conversations, checking for the usage of unkind words in households. He would visit bars to scan for fights and riots. By doing so, he learnt about the struggles people endured; parents arguing about how to pay the week's rent, partners fighting among each other about dishonesty, and teens strategizing about mischief. As his visits increased, the king became more and more aware about the unkindness and unhappiness in his kingdom.

He spent sleepless nights yearning to change this, to help everybody, to feel the vibrant glow of happiness spread through his

BHANTE SARANAPALA

kingdom. He endured countless sleepless nights, devising a method of helping people to find the path of kindfulness and happiness. On one of these nights he realized that before attempting to help other people change and gain a kind perspective and kind intention, he too must have a kind perspective and kind intention. He also realized that his ministers and advisors must have an equally kindful intention and perspective to spread happiness as he does. With a smile on his face, he was able to calmly drift off to sleep that hopeful night.

The next morning he called a mandatory meeting for all of the people in his court. After everyone was present, he calmly began explaining how he wanted everyone in the kingdom to be happy and kind to one another. He explained how they should be kind to everyone in the kingdom despite their economic status, race, gender, sexual orientation, or (dis)abilities. He taught them about how kind perspective and kind intention can be used to make a happier kingdom with no violence or unkindness. Finally, he stated, "As the leaders of this kingdom, we must first gain this kind intention and kind perspective. We must want to help people and spread happiness. We must refrain from harming people. Especially people who have harmed us or other people and living beings. We shall learn how to spread this kindful intention and perspective of harmlessness throughout this kingdom. We can ensure the rise of a happy and kind kingdom, yet this has to start from us. Who would like to help me to do this?" A moment of deafening silence filled the courtroom as the gravity of his request settled in. They thought of a kinder place where people did not hurt anybody, where there were no disputes, no murders, no theft. They thought of how beautiful and peaceful living in such a place would be. One by one, they were filled with the good intention and perspective to help create this realm of happiness.

With the help of his ministers and advisors, the king was able to assist people like never before. They visited people in need, spread care packages for the homeless, listened to the struggles of the average citizen, and helped them find creative solutions to their problems. They used kindness to open the eyes of greedy landowners to see that their tenants were struggling. They gave people who had committed crimes an opportunity to change and live a better life, showing forgiveness rather than punishment. They even helped people in the far corners of the kingdom, giving them access to clean water and fresh food. Soon, the people in the kingdom realized the king and his ministers were helping them, which gave them a sense of ease and union. They began working together, helping each other to reach success. Without having the landlords breathing down their necks, the farmers were able to calmly and kindfully plant their crops. Thus, their harvest became more prosperous. With their yield, they were able to pay back all of the missed rent to the landlord. With a plentiful harvest, they were also able to share some food with homeless and marginally housed people so that they were not starving. With the new found energy provided from the food, they were able to begin working and earning for themselves, and could focus on securing housing without having to wonder where they would get their next meal. Everybody was caught with the strong bond of kindfulness, and soon everybody in the kingdom was happy, calm, and peaceful. Yet, the power of such kindfulness did not stop there. It spread to the animals, trees, and other living beings. Trees became greener and more fruitful, and animals and insects no longer had to dine on the crops of farmers but had plentiful food from the wild trees. The king's wish had come true! Everybody in his kingdom was happy and had kindful perspectives and intentions.

The Roots of Relationships:
Kind Speech, Kind Action, and Kind Livelihood

The three roots of the roots of relationships are active manifestations of your intentions. They are the wholesome desire to not cause suffering to yourself or others. They are the active and self-reinforcing realization that you can be a source of happiness for all that enter and surround your lives. Going beyond mental attitudes and intentions, you act, say, and do things in a way that creates a positive impact and a peaceful social environment. They are self-reinforcing in the sense that the things you say and do become a reflection of who you are as a human being.

You can have many wonderful and pleasant ideas about the kind of person you would like to be in the future. For example, "I want to be rich, live in a big mansion, and drive a fast car." Or, "I wish that the way my parents raised me hadn't caused me all of these problems." Embracing kind speech, kind action, and kind livelihood, however, allow you to act, right here in the present moment. This allows you to live in a way that creates the joy, peace, and happiness you want to have in your life, despite what your external circumstances may be at this particular point in time. This is not a passive form of wishful thinking that everything will be fine irrespective of you. Rather, it is actively taking charge of your life by saying and doing that which will actualize your kind view and kind intention. By doing so, this will ultimately result in you being happy in the present moment, not in some idealized future that may or may not exist.

Kind speech can take many forms; it can be as simple as a "thank you" or larger as in an open, honest, and vulnerable conversation with someone who is dear to you. In all of its forms, grand or small, kind speech has certain traits. It is honest, free of gossip, and done to benefit you or others. It is something to be thoroughly explored by looking at your own life. What happens when you speak in a way that is harsh or divisive? What does that do to your relationships? What does it do to your mind and the way you perceive the world?

Frequently, I provide counselling services to families going through division and strife. One of the common behaviours I witness is the breakdown of kind speech. Before long, a wife is recounting how her husband shouted at her or the husband accuses his wife of belittling him. The children are telling lies and being deceitful, or one partner is cheating on the other. This concealment, dishonesty, or harsh speech, though tempting in the moment, creates an atmosphere of anger, frustration, and mistrust.

To assess whether your speech was kind, observe both the effects of your speech and the intentions you had before you spoke. Were your intentions kind or harmful?

Children are taught to say "Thank you" when receiving treats. When you say, "Thank you," are you saying thank you with your lips, or are you saying thank you with your heart? Do you feel gratitude before you say thank you?

Humans have a tendency to enjoy unkind speech, such as lying, swearing, and gossiping. Though you may recognize that it is harmful to others, if you are not mindful, you may develop habits of harmful speech. Train yourself to speak kind and meaningful words, and refrain from using unkind words. Notice the happiness you gain from engaging in conversations that are a source of peace and harmony rather than sadness and disharmony. If you are stuck in the cycle of harm produced by lying, try to break that cycle by reflecting with kind perspective and kind intention. Use your understanding of cause and effect to change and transform your speech into honest, kind, less harmful forms. Take your reflection as an opportunity for self-transformation. Identify what type of person you want to be, what type of speech you want engage in with the people around you.

Kind Action means "walk the talk." Witnessing hypocrisy in others can evoke anger or frustration. It can be upsetting to see a wealthy individual say it's important to improve the well-being of a country and then watch them sail off in their yacht or fly away in their private jet.

Kind action is about going beyond your speech and intentions. It's about doing what will benefit you and others. It can be overwhelming and disheartening, at times, to think about the unkind actions humans do to each other. It can be tempting to believe that the world can be fixed by changing everything around you. Even if the world and your own life seems out of control, you can still control your own actions. You can choose to act in a way that benefits both you and others.

More than two decades ago, I started a soup kitchen program at a shelter in Toronto. Hoping to inspire the community to action and instill positive values, I reached out to young people in my network to gauge their interest in volunteering. They jumped at the opportunity to help and even enthusiastically showed up early at the shelter. Of course, that never happened. Getting them to participate was like pulling teeth. Why would teens and young adults want to give up time playing video games or socializing with friends to wake up early on a weekend and volunteer their time? Nevertheless, I was able to convince a few teens into attending with me. I encouraged them to treat the users of the shelter like distinguished guests as these people were already facing unkindness, discrimination, physical insecurity, and emotional distress on a daily basis. Why not be the one face of kindness that they would look forward to seeing?

The youth got fired up and took up my challenge and truly honoured the presence of everyone, warmly welcoming them and graciously serving them. It was five-star service at its best.

After running this program for a while, I began to notice a shift. Where previously securing volunteers was a struggle, some young people began to return week after week. More noticeably, some of their friends joined them. Eventually, as the list of volunteers grew longer, I had to schedule volunteers and even had to turn some away occasionally.

So why would young people busy socializing, preparing for exams, and working at part-time jobs take time from their personal lives to help at a shelter during the weekend? The debrief stories were telling and quite common. Their initial feelings of apprehension and uncertainty quickly turned to joy and happiness when they helped someone else in need. The youth who continued returning week after week expressed that this joy grew exponentially, making them appreciative and content, to the point that they would look forward to their days at the shelter. It became apparent that kind actions breed happiness.

If you ever find yourself feeling down, a helpful solution can be to do something for someone else. Being generous can pull you out of your habitual thought pattern and expand your awareness to encompass people around you. It builds meaningful human connections and reduces your sense of alienation and separation.

Kind action can also be about restraint or restriction. Consider the following. Suppose a person wakes up in the middle of the night to use the washroom, only to stub their toe on their night table. Clutching their foot in pain and cursing as they hobble over to the bathroom, they think about what a fool they are. A few nights later, the same person stubs their toe yet again. This happens on a third night, after which this tired, angry individual resigns to do something about it. The next day, they begin rolling out of bed on the left side of the bed instead of the right. Problem solved. The lesson is, if you do something repeatedly and produce the same result, then it's time you start thinking about doing something different.

If you know that taking drugs, consuming large amounts of alcohol, or being unfaithful results in you vomiting, alienating others, or hurting your partner and feeling extreme regret and guilt, you need to make an effort toward restraint. These are actions that result in psychological or physical harm to you or others, whether immediately or in the long term. Kindful action is refraining from negative actions.

However, restraint is only one aspect when reflecting on kind action. You should also actively nurture kind action, even in the face of discomfort. This allows you to replace negative habits with positive ones. For example, you can nurture life by protecting the sanctity of another's life or by voting for candidates who support minority rights and pressuring your elected officials to do more to advance access to equitable care and services for populations facing barriers. You can build relationships committed to honesty and trust, nurturing healthy relationships without violence or infidelity. You can be more mindful of what you put into your body and ensure that you only consume what helps you remain healthy, aware, and alert and eat in a way that is the most sustainable.

How do you know if something is really beneficial to you and others? You cannot simply trust your own opinion. Opinions are fluid and change with time. If you reflect on decisions you made as a child or as a teenager, you might sheepishly grin at how stupid you were. And yet, at the time your opinions would have justified those actions. So, then, what should you do?

You have the benefit of having a body with which to experience the sensory world and a mind with which to reflect upon that experience. In looking at negative actions to avoid and positive ones to nurture, reflect on how these relate to your own sensory experience. To help break negative habits, you should always ensure that you take time for introspective reflection.

This is where kind perspective and kind intention come in. By reflecting on the effects of your actions, similar to your reflections on the effects of your speech, you'll begin to reinforce positive behaviours that produce beneficial results. You'll let go of old, habitual patterns that hamper your journey toward happiness and peace. At times, you may not like what you find. Habits you may be very attached to might be the very ones that are providing you with a false sense of comfort, reinforcing your unhappiness. This is why you can see hundreds of people an hour via YouTube and yet feel lonelier than ever.

You may find great happiness in recollecting kind actions you have done for others or that others have done for you. Think about how many individuals had to have helped you in some way for you to be where you are today. Everyone from the farmer who harvested the food on your plate to your parents or guardians who cared for you to the best of their abilities. Reflect on how many individuals have refrained from unkind actions.

Canada has relative political stability and is not in a state of war. You can come and go freely for the most part and often do not have to worry about a stranger harming you. This is the result of refraining from unkind actions, such as harming others. During the COVID pandemic, think about how many lives were saved as a result of the kindness of doctors and nurses putting their own lives at risk. In this way, kind action produces great societal benefit, and reflecting regularly on kind action arouses joy and happiness in the mind.

The following story shows the importance of a kind livelihood and the effects of not having one.

The Sage, the Pig Farmer, and His Nightmares

Once there was a wise elder who was travelling to a small urban town named Bellville. As she travelled she encountered a farmer, who invited her over for coffee. The wise elder gratefully accepted the offer, as she was growing weary from her travels. She followed the man up to the farm, and upon their arrival at the dim and sooty farm, the farmer began making coffee and invited the elder to sit down. While sitting, the elder calmly observed the bareness of the living room, and as her knowing gaze scanned the room, she came across the tired and helpless demeanour of the farmer. As the farmer finished preparing the coffee and presented it to the elder, she asked the farmer if he was doing okay. The farmer replied by saying, "Unfortunately I am not, dear elder, for I've not been able to sleep for weeks now. Every time I try to sleep, I see these terrifying nightmares. I end up waking in a fit in the middle of the night sweating, too terrified to go to sleep again." The elder took a sip of her coffee as she pondered this. "What happens in these nightmares? Do you have the same one, or different ones?" she queried. After a moment of reflection, the farmer began depicting his nightmares.

"I get different nightmares each time, but it's always the same ending. A couple of days ago, I dreamed that I had shrunk to the size of a pig and the pigs had grown to the size of me. It was almost as if we had switched places. There was this particularly burly, mean-looking pig, and he had these long pointy forks in his hands and this evil grin as he advanced on me. I tried screaming, and calling for help, but nobody could hear me because I could only squeal, like a pig. So, I squealed helplessly, only to be poked relentlessly by that pig. Then, I could somehow see them cooking me for dinner. THEY MADE ME INTO STEW! I could only watch as they drank me, while commenting on how delicious I was." The man paused to finish his coffee, tears accumulating in his eyes as

he recounted the nightmare he had the previous night, his hands shaking as he brought the cup to his lips, only to spill several drops and hastily dab it up with his napkin. "Last night, the same thing happened, but they strangled me instead and made me into pork chops. Oh, please tell me, what should I do to get rid of these bad dreams?" the man pleaded.

"May I ask what you farm?" the elder asked, beginning to comprehend the issue. "Well, I farm pigs. It's what my family has been doing for a long time now," the man replies. After hearing this, the elder replied, "See dear farmer. That is your issue. Through pig farming, you murder helpless animals as a source of food and profit. You have experienced their pain first-hand through your nightmares. Therefore, in order for your nightmares to cease, you must stop killing pigs." Realization dawned upon the farmer as he acknowledged this, "But wise one, how will I survive if I sell my farm, I will starve!"

"Not to fear, you are welcome at the community I am residing in. It is in Bellville. Yet, do not rush your decision. I will leave you to your thoughts, and if you decide to do so, you can travel and meditate with me." With that, the elder stood up, thanked the farmer for his hospitality and left the man to collect his thoughts.

After several more sleepless nights, and terrifying nightmares, the farmer made up his mind, sold his farm and stopped killing pigs as the elder suggested. Then, he set out to seek the elder's company at her site of spiritual worship in Bellville. There he meditated and developed mindfulness and kindness. While doing so, he noticed that the nightmares became less scary and even reduce in quantity. The elder was correct! He could finally get some sleep. He happily informed the elder that the nightmares had reduced in intensity and frequency. The elder smiled at this news and replied, "If you want to stop having nightmares all together, try and release the pigs that are going to be killed. Here are some donations I have received; you may take them with you." With faith in the elder, the *man set off the next day with the donations in search of more pig farms. He was able to visit three pig farms and was able to save over fifty lives. With each one he saved, his happiness grew, and a sense of lightness and serenity flooded him as he smiled from ear to ear. At the end of the day, he returned to the monastery and was welcomed with the warm embrace of a good night's sleep. Just as the elder had said, his nightmares were gone forever.*

Yet, the man grew to enjoy doing such kindful deeds and eventually became a farmer again. He would grow fruits and vegetables of all shapes, sizes, and colours. He would feed the homeless, seniors, and animals. He would see the smiles of the people and beings he served and that would fill him up with such pleasure, that not only did he eliminate his nightmares, but he began having positive dreams of all the good deeds he was doing in the world. Oftentimes, he still visits the monastery in Bellville where he meditates with the elder. He realizes a person's livelihood has significantly impacts their happiness. When he was a pig farmer, he was very unhappy and had terrible nightmares, yet now, his farm is a source of happiness.

This story exposes one of the many forms of unkindful livelihoods or occupations. You may have seen, heard about, or experienced the effects of such occupations in your everyday life, like human trafficking, drug trafficking, arms dealing, or other illegal activities. In these livelihoods, a person makes money from harming other living beings. Though these livelihoods may provide a lofty profit, the person accumulates a more significant amount of guilt. Additionally, many of these unkindful livelihoods are illegal around the world, though some are not.

How do you know if you are living a kind livelihood? How can you properly discern what is kind and unkind? First, you must avoid engaging in any livelihood that involves the trading of living beings, weapons, flesh, and addictive substances, such alcohol, drugs, or poison. By doing so, you can ensure that you are doing a kindful occupation. If your livelihood does involve one of these trades, you can still change your occupation using these steps:

Step 1: Reflect

Before changing your career path, understand clearly the need for that change. Mindfully reflect on your current career using kind perspective. Without judgment, determine whether your work is harming people. If you are a bartender, you are selling alcohol to people. In turn, your customers may experience physical effects on their health and increased risk of violence and abuse. Your customers may also encounter psychological and relationship issues. If you are aware of these negative consequences, you may begin experiencing the guilt of selling those intoxicants. If you are working in a job where you are asked to do unethical things, such as defraud people by taking advantage of the elderly, you may get similar signs from your body and your mind that tell you that this is not OK. You may experience stress, anxiety, or emotional exhaustion. These are all warnings that your work is not kindful and that you should change it.

Step 2: Develop

After reflecting and understanding that you need to change your unkind existing occupation, you must develop a method to do so using the roots of wisdom, kind perspective, and kind intention. Decide first which occupation you have the qualifications for or for which you can readily obtain appropriate qualifications through training or education. Then reflect on whether that job is harmful to any living being using kind perspective.

For instance, if you have the qualifications to become a barista, think of the cause and effect surrounding that occupation. By selling coffee and morning snacks, or breakfast, you will be able to feed people on their way to work and bring joy to brighten their mornings before the long commute. Therefore, your job is kindful, as it is helping people and spreading happiness in some small way.

After deciding which occupation you want to apply for, you should apply at different places that have availability for that position and accept the offer that makes you the happiest. Then, you can leave the position you deemed unkind. By doing so, you will reduce your guilt as you know that you are no longer harming anyone for your personal benefit.

Along with a kindful livelihood, you must also conduct it kindfully. Using kindful intention, set a goal to perform your work so that it produces happiness for yourself, your employers, and your clients. Develop the intention to speak and act in a way that is kindful and does not harm anyone. In the case of the barista, welcome your customers with an enthusiastic smile, fill their order to the best of your ability, and have them leave with a happy smile themselves. Furthermore, knowing that you tried your best at work and that you spread smiles throughout your day will be happiness in itself. This will ensure that you enjoy and look forward to your work. As you continue handing out coffee and cookies and sharing smiles, you will be flooded with joy and happiness. No doubt you may encounter problems or issues, yet by using your happiness, you will be able to work through them.

Despite finding this happiness, you may still feel slightly guilty, knowing that there are other bartenders who may not recognize the consequences of their actions and continue to serve alcohol to customers. You might get nightmares here and there, with people cursing you for the negative energy you spread from your previous occupation. This is where the third step of this cycle comes into play.

Step 3: Nurture and Maintain

Just as the sage advised the pig farmer to free some captured pigs, you too must develop kindful actions. In the case of a bartender, you could advise people against drinking and you could donate money to people who lost someone to alcohol. You could help people to find more kindful occupations. By doing so, you can prevent others from experiencing unhappiness caused by their job. You must also remember to continue nurturing these deeds with kindful action, kindful speech, and kindful intention.

The Roots of Awareness: Kind Effort, Kind Mindfulness, and Kind Stillness

The roots of awareness help strengthen the previous two sets of roots of the Kindful Tree: the roots of wisdom and the roots of relationships. The roots of awareness provide valuable insight and feedback about your own lived experience, which supports both wisdom and relationships. Your wisdom allows you to delve further into awareness—knowing when to watch out for traps and pitfalls—and your relationships support this deep internal reflection, allowing you to feel safe and held, while holding up a mirror to your current state of mind. In other words, a feedback loop exists between all three roots.

Kind effort is the energy you expend to put your kind intention into action. While you have kind intention to implement in order to benefit yourself and others and refrain from unkind actions, you must also use kind effort to act on this intention.

You need to use kind perspective and kind intention to prevent yourself from conducting unkind actions. The following story illustrates this.

The Hawk and the Quail

One day a quail wanted to go out of its proper territory, the territory where all quails feel safe. His colleague quails warned him to not go out of this territory, because the quail baby would be a victim of hawks. Despite the warning, the quail went out roaming. As he started roaming, the hawk saw the quail, swooped down and grabbed the quail with its paws. As it was being carried out to the nest of the hawk, the quail started crying aloud saying, "It is my bad luck that I did not listen to my colleagues. If I listened to their words and stayed in our proper territory, this hawk, our enemy, wouldn't be a match for me and he couldn't have grabbed me." Then the hawk asked the quail, "What is your proper territory?" The quail said, "Mr. Hawk, our proper territory is the field, newly plowed, with clumps of earth all turned up."

The hawk, without boasting of its strength and confidence, told the quail, "You quail, I release you now. I let you go to your territory. But remember that even there I can come and grab you, if I want." So, the quail was released. The quail went to its own territory and tested the strength of the hawk. The quail stood up on the top of the clump of earth and taunted and screamed saying, "Mr. Hawk, if possible, now come and grab me." The hawk folded its wings and swooped down with full speed to grab the quail. As the hawk was approaching with full speed, the quail went inside the newly-plowed clump earth. The hawk, not being able to catch the quail, hit the newly plowed clump earth and hurt himself badly. The hawk could not grab the quail.

If we stay in our territory, nobody can grab and hurt us. We will not be victims to anyone. In the story the quail is in improper territory, a hostile, unfriendly, and unkind environment where everyone feels unsafe. Hawks are hovering around in the sky and they are looking for quails and other prey. If they see quails, they are going to get them. However, if the quails stay in the newly-plowed field, in the safe, friendly, and kind environment, they be safe, and will not become victims to the hawks.

Our proper, friendly and kind territory is the present moment, it is our safe territory.

By receding into kindfulness, you will prevent yourself from engaging in unkindful actions. If you choose to engage in unkindful actions and speech, you might win a few battles but eventually you will hurt yourself and others. By choosing to prioritize kindful actions and speak kindful words, you avoid harming yourself and others. You might not be perfect however over time, you will develop the wisdom to deal with difficulties, assess the situation, and decide how to act.

Not only should you strive to prevent conducting negative actions in the future, you should also understand and let go of unkind feelings or habits that already occur. This does not mean suppressing, denying or developing hatred toward your unkind qualities. Rather, it means bringing an attitude of kind curiosity to where the dark places of your mind are—the flaws you might not want to look at—and figuring out how they might be harming you or others.

Reflect and identify these unkind habits and their origin. Reflect on the effect of these unkind habits and how they harm you and others. When you feel the urge to indulge in such habits, see if you can mindfully maintain your kind perspective and kind intention. Over time, as you continue with this effort, the harmful habits of unhappiness will disappear. Do not become angry or disappointed if your habit does not break overnight as some of these habits have accumulated over many years. Instead, persist with a steady flow of kindfulness.

While making a kind effort to cultivate kind deeds, kind words, and kind thoughts that you do not already have, also make a kind effort to further enhance those you have by taking additional action with more kind deeds.

Kind mindfulness is the ability to remain in the present, using kind effort to reflect on your state of being at any particular moment. Kind mindfulness allows you to notice and recall your current state, appreciating what you have while still noticing what needs to be tended to. In this way, you are able to refrain from engaging in unkindful actions and become able to be kindful in the present. You can maintain this with:

Mindfulness of Your Body and Your Five Senses

In order to truly understand the relationship between certain mental states, bodily actions, speech, and your well-being, you must be mindful of your body's physical sensations. When observing, you must do so mindfully and in the present.

You can use kindful intention to observe and notice the good qualities in things that you may not have seen before. For example, notice how when you feel alive and are happy, the sky looks bluer and the bird's chirping sounds more beautiful to you. Where did this blue sky go when you were depressed? Why did the bird's chirping sound different? These beautiful things and sounds did not disappear. Beauty is always accessible; however, it is your state of mind that sometimes closes you off to the experience of beauty. With mindfulness, you can learn how to experience life to the fullest and kindest in the present moment.

You can start by being mindful of your breath. Most of the time, you are not aware that you are breathing. By focusing on this small action, it will be easier for you when making important decisions. This habit can be further developed through a mindfulness meditation practice, which is covered in other chapters.

By being mindful of your body and your senses, you can prevent yourself from losing control over your actions. If you are not mindful, you may cause harm to others when you feel that your body is being harmed. When you experience something unpleasant, you may become surrounded by unkind thoughts. To prevent this, be mindful when these thoughts occur so that you can stop from acting on them.

Mindfulness of Your Feelings and Emotions

When experiencing daily life, be mindful of your feelings and of your emotions. The two are inseparable from your daily experience because you always feel something. You should recognize whether you are having a pleasant, unpleasant, or neutral feeling about something. By doing so, you can ensure that you maintain kind intention and kind perspective toward your feelings, rather than trying to always control or be enslaved by them. Instead, you want to able to gain perspective on your feelings and emotions. Without perspective, if you do not recognize your emotion and regain control of yourself when you experience strong emotions of unpleasantness, you may hurt others around you.

You can do this by focusing on the emotions as they arise in you. This can be easy or difficult, depending on the situation. If you are in a situation where you are being hurt, you may easily notice feelings of unpleasantness as they arise. If someone gives you a present that you really like, then you will notice a pleasant feeling. Knowing the state of your emotions allows you to gain perspective and make good choices on how to act, rather than merely being controlled and reacting to your emotions.

Mindfulness of the Five Hurdles

The five hurdles are sensual craving, anger, laziness, agitation, and doubt. These internal hurdles weaken your mind's capacity to understand with wisdom the power of kindfulness. They obstruct the evolution of your mind toward full awakening with kindness. With kindful mindfulness, reflect on these hurdles as they can weaken your perspective and intentions, causing unhappiness and disrupting your peace.

When observing your emotions and feelings, be mindful of the causes of your feelings and emotions to help give you insight into your actions. If the cause of your actions or emotions are one or more of the five hurdles—sensual craving, anger, laziness, agitation, doubt—reflect on the consequences of such emotions and actions.

All three forms of kind mindfulness work interdependently as you go about your day. You might act in a way that causes an unpleasant feeling, which in turn causes one of the five hurdles. If you are not kindful about these things, they can cause unwanted unhappiness. You must learn how to do so in a collective method so that you are able to be completely in the present and know what you are experiencing both physically and emotionally.

Kind stillness is using kind effort, kind intention, and kind mindfulness to gain and maintain a calm, peaceful, and still mind and life. Kind stillness is bolstered by your ability to speak, act, and engage in a livelihood that is kindful because by living this way, your mind rids itself of any guilt or doubt about how you relate to the world. With this self-assured, peaceful, kind, and still mind, you will be able to gain true happiness.

Through meditation and the cultivation of all roots of the Kindful Tree, you will be able to free your mind from pain and unkindness to prevent unhappiness. You must recognize that unwholesome and unhappy emotions, thoughts, and actions disrupt this stillness. This is why it is important to maintain this peacefulness with kindness and love. If you are not able to do that, it will be easier for your unhappy mind to cause unhappiness in yourself and in others. And if you are unhappy with your life, the sight of others being happy will cause you anger. Consequently, you are more likely to harm that person and spread more unhappiness, which is not beneficial for you or others.

However, if you have a still mind, your demeanour, speech, and actions will reflect stillness. You may experience greater calm and relaxation, and it may be easier for you to interact and speak with others because you are able to listen to them with an open and kind mind.

Since your thoughts are the basis for most of your actions, you must realize that by developing harmful thoughts, you are more likely to harm yourself and others. That is why you should reflect on your thoughts to check if they are unwholesome, as these unwholesome thoughts are unhealthy to you and others. You must also take action to free your mind from such thoughts, otherwise they will grow and consume your whole mind.

To do this, first learn to recognize an unwholesome thought. An unwholesome thought is based on self-centredness that invokes feelings such as greed, hatred, aversion, jealousy, envy, conceit, pride, ego, and stinginess. With reflection, you can easily understand how these emotions disturb your peace of mind, cause unhappiness, and harm people.

When acknowledging the presence of these unhappy thoughts, be mindful that they do not grow and cause unhappiness. Your mind is like your house, and you must ensure that its calmness is not taken over by unwelcome intruders. You must be alert to someone attempting to break in; they will hide when you double-check that nobody is there. Also be mindful to recognize that those intruders might attempt to break in again. You must, yet again, double-check that nobody is there. Eventually, after this cycle repeats a couple more times, the intruder will become tired of trying to break in and will leave. By simply being mindful and making an effort to check for the presence of a harmful intruder, you have prevented an intrusion into the stillness of your mind.

This mindfulness will prevent the growth of unwholesome thoughts. Yet, to regain your stillness and rid your mind of such thoughts, you must cultivate kind thoughts that make your mind happy. If you have thoughts of greed, you must learn to develop kind thoughts of giving. Just as we feed a baby when it is hungry so that it does not remain hungry, you must feed your brain with kindful thoughts so that the harmful thoughts do not remain. By feeding your minds healthy, kind, compassionate, and wholesome thoughts, you can free your mind from unwholesome thoughts. By having a mind that is free from unwholesome thoughts—like greed, anger, jealousy, stinginess, and selfishness—you can maintain a still mind and are then also able to maintain a happy mind and a happy life.

Preparing the mind for this type of development requires the prevention of unwholesome thoughts, speech, and action; the elimination of existing ones; the nurturing of existing positive states of mind; and the planting of the seed for new positive states to arise. The tree of happiness cannot survive and bear fruit from the nutrients provided from one root; it needs the nutrients provided from many roots combined.

Throughout this chapter, I have discussed at length the roots of awareness and attempted to demonstrate how the three roots interrelate to form a path to personal peace, well-being, and emotional safety. I encourage you to revisit this and other chapters when you encounter challenges or when you feel you need more clarity on where you are going. You may find new insights and ways of cultivating the three roots that did not immediately jump out to you the first time around, or you may recognize things that have become relevant because your state of mind and the challenges you are working with have changed. It is through critical, intentional, and repeated reflection that you can arrive at the place of inner peace and be a source of kindfulness for yourself and others.

CHAPTER 14

Kindfulness and Interdependency

"Interdependence is and ought to be as much the ideal of man as self-sufficiency. Man is a social being."

— MAHATMA GANDHI

In this era, where you can communicate across the world at the click of a button, the concept of interdependence is becoming more and more alien. Reliant on technology, some people stop recognizing that there are humans behind the screens. Cybercrime and cyber bullying have increased as people become infatuated with getting away with crime when online. They feel untouchable and engage in unkind actions on social media platforms. Despite temporarily feeling rushes of power, people tend to feel lonelier and more isolated. Even if you do not engage in cyberbullying or cybercrime, you may still experience this isolation, loneliness, and disconnection from the world. These feelings were made worse during the COVID-19 restrictions.

More than ever, you depend on technology to do simple day-to-day tasks like shopping, ordering food, even talking with nearby family and friends. By doing so, you fail to realize that there people like farmers, office employees, and couriers behind our shipments. Though technology has carried many industries through the pandemic, it has also made genuine connection more remote.

Kindfulness to Yourself and Others

Though you may not realize it, your happiness and harmony rely on other people performing their duties. In return, other people's happiness and harmony rely on the performance of your duties. If you are not happy and do not fulfill your various roles of mother/father, employee/employer, or child with care, others will be impacted negatively. You can see this in families when parents are unhappy and distraught; their children will likely be angry and distraught as well. That is why you must remember to be kindful to yourself and to others.

If you are not happy, calm, and kind, the people around you cannot be happy, calm, and kind. You are given similar instructions in the case of an emergency on an airplane. You are told to put your oxygen mask on first before helping others with theirs.

I would like to share a story about the Zulu phrase, Ubuntu, which has roots in the humanist African philosophy of community being integral to society. This phrase displays the extent to which our well-being depends on others' well-being.

Ubuntu

There once was a vast mountain area filled with lush beautiful trees, sparkling aquamarine creaks, and shallow flowing rivers and waterfalls. Some trees grew dozens of meters tall, while others were barely taller than a child. Yet, each one had a different type of fruit; some were sweet and small, others were plump and luscious. Among these trees lived bright, colourful birds of all sizes and shapes. You could see them fluttering around, pecking at whatever fruit they desired. After receiving a filling meal, they would sing enchanting songs and melodies that could be heard from miles below in the small village at the foothill of the mountain. The families in this village would climb the mountain to bathe in the freshwater creeks and rivers. The adults would take showers under the waterfalls, listening to the calming sound of rushing water above them as they did so. The children would spend hours on end after school, staring at the sparkling rocks at the bottom of the creeks as they glimmered in the sunshine. The colour of the rocks would change colours as the sun went down and the voices of their parents could be heard from below, calling them to come down for dinner.

On one fateful day, an anthropologist came upon this village as he was travelling. After observing the village and the lifestyle of the villagers for a couple of days, he decided that this was the perfect place for him to conduct some research for his latest study. The next morning, he called all of the children in the village to gather around him. When they were all present, he showed them the pristine giant of the mountain. "I need all of you to line up at the edge of this mountain. On the count of three, I want you all to run up this mountain as fast as you can. Whoever reaches the top of the mountain will be the owner of the mountain and all of the luxuries that come with the mountain. All of it will be yours, if you get there first!" With the ownership of the mountain at stake, and tension flying sky high, the children lined up at the bottom within an arms-length apart from each other. "1 . . . 2 . . . 3!" exclaimed the man, sending the children flying past him and up the mountain.

From above, you could see the relatives of each child hoping and praying for their child to climb faster, yelling words of enthusiasm, and urging the children to run faster and more vigilantly. The anthropologist marvelled at the speed of the children. As he observed them, he noticed that one kid was almost at the top and was running faster with a steadier pace than the rest of the children. All of a sudden, he stopped. Exclamations of surprise aroused among the onlookers, as his family yelled at him to continue, to reach the top and earn the mountain. "EVERYBODY STOP!" the boy yelled, catching the attention of all of the children, stopping them in their tracks. The audience watched in amazement as all of them joined hands. "Let us climb this mountain together, that way we can all have this mountain," the boy said, as they began climbing together. Shouts of acknowledgment aroused from the bottom of the mountain, as they cheered on all of the children. After what seemed like a century, all of the children stopped and turned around to face the bottom, they had reached the top together. They all owned the mountain and everybody had access to the beautiful fruits and clear waters. Everybody was happy, parents embraced their children as they came back down, smiling from ear to ear.

After the excitement of the moment had passed, the anthropologist called the kid who introduced the idea of reaching the top together. "Why did you decide that everybody should reach the top together?" the man asked the boy. The boy smiled and replied, "Ubuntu." "Ubuntu?" the anthropologist questioned, even more confused. The boy nodded, "Ubuntu, it means, I am, because we are." Then he explained, "As I was running up that mountain, I realized how sad I would be if I did not get to the top first. I knew I was ahead of everybody else, and I felt sad for them. I realized that some of them were my friends that I play with on that mountain. I thought about how they would not be able to play with me if I reached the top alone which would make them unhappy. I also realized that if they were unhappy, I would be unhappy as well. That is why I decided that we would all climb the

mountain together and reach the top together." The anthropologist
pondered this concept for a moment, astonished about the wisdom
this boy had. "Thank you for explaining. I understand now," said
the anthropologist, as he perceived the strength of interdependency
that lived in this village.

Just as the boy's kindfulness and sense of interdependency
was able to ensure that everybody in his village was happy,
we must also recognize this interdependency. We must realize
that if we are not happy, we cannot spread happiness to others.
Just as the boy first got ahead before stopping the others, we
must attain kindfulness before spreading kindfulness. To attain
this kindfulness, we must use the practices outlined in chapter
seven to go past the self-centered thoughts and actions as these
thoughts can harm us and, through cause and effect, harm all of
the people surrounding us.

We must perceive everyone as friends and family. This doesn't
mean you have to like everyone—and indeed there are many
members within families who don't like each other. But it does
mean that we have to strive for a deeper understanding of our
dependence on one another and, consequently, the need to
accept one another because of this very interdependence. We
must understand this interconnection. Yet, we cannot do so
without cultivating a deeper consciousness.

By developing this deeper consciousness, we will be able to
transform our actions from selfish and exclusive actions to selfless
and inclusive actions. We must realize that exclusion will harm
us. Similarly, the harm created from exclusion will damage our
coexistence with those we depend on. Contrarily, the cultivation
of selflessness and inclusion will help us develop an appreciation
of the reality of this coexistence—a reality that exists regardless of whether we choose to acknowledge it. Acknowledging

our interdependency does not create something that wasn't there to begin with; rather, it wakes us up to living in a way that acknowledges that which is always present. It will make our coexistence easier and more fruitful for us and the people we are coexisting with.

CHAPTER 15

The Practice of Kindful
Interdependency

"The fundamental law of human beings is interdependence. A person is a person through other persons."

—DESMOND TUTU

In order to cultivate selfless and inclusive thoughts, speech, action, and personality, you must be mindful of the moments when your behaviour or your actions are harming someone. When you realize that you are causing harm, it is helpful to take the attitude that the person you are harming is a person you care deeply about—such as your mother, father, friend, or relative—as this attitude will prevent you from inflicting further unhappiness. For instance, if you notice anger arising when the waitress spills coffee on you by accident, first become mindful of your anger. Then cultivate the kindness aspect of kindfulness by imagining that person as a relative or friend. By doing so, you prevent yourself from causing harm as you realize that by harming a relative or friend, you would be harming yourself as well. This helps deepen your sense of interdependency.

When you have developed a deeper appreciation of interdependency, what then? We are all interconnected, but how do you relate to this reality? To cultivate this interdependency, practise the following four principles in a kindful manner.

Practise Giving

The act of giving helps you cultivate selflessness. Every time you give, your yearning to give increases and you progressively become more selfless and less selfish. With fewer selfish thoughts to plague your actions and speech, you can attain happiness yourself and also spread happiness to everyone around you.

At first, it may be difficult for you to give or to recognize the selfish thoughts that prevent you from giving. You may think, "Is giving to this person worth it?" or "What do I get from giving to this person?" Sometimes it may seem like it's not worth giving if you do not get anything back, especially if the person has been unkind to you. Be mindful of such thoughts and actively work to stop them. Such thoughts can give rise to a strong sense of hatred and unhappiness. To prevent this, give to someone, no matter who the person is, as long as you have the capacity to do so. Realize that it matters not who you give to. Simply give selflessly, without wanting or expecting anything in return. This capacity to give is available even if you do not have material things, as you can give a smile, a helping hand, or a kind ear.

By giving, you will always gain something even if you do not always realize it at the time. It's precious when you realize that you made someone happy. They may not show their happiness on the outside, but if you give to them kindfully, they will always be happy on the inside.

It is very important to give kindfully because if you do not give kindfully, you will be spreading unhappiness instead of happiness. In order to give kindfully, remind yourself of your kind intention. This kind intention ensures that you and the recipient are both happy. If you give while you are angry or still attached to the item you are giving, you will be unhappy giving, and the recipient will likely be unhappy receiving it. With kind intention, you become mindful to give something that is beneficial to that person.

Often, selflessness can be developed through a cyclical process. By giving, you become less selfish, and by becoming less selfish, you give more. When beginning with this cycle of giving, give something that you are not very attached to. As you progressively develop this practice of giving, you will become less attached to your things and your belongings. Then you will be able to give something you are attached to for the well-being and happiness of another person.

The following story by Ajahn Brahm demonstrates how an act of kindfulness gives back, as it always does.

Milk & Cookies

There once was a poor medical student who had to do odd jobs to pay for college. One such job that he did was as a door-to-door salesman. After a long day without any sales, he knocked on yet another door to try and sell something. A woman answered the door and listened to his sales pitch after which she declined to buy anything. However, before he could leave, she noticed how tired he seemed and asked if he had eaten anything. To this he replied that he had not. "Wait here, I will bring you something to eat," the woman said out of kindfulness as she disappeared behind the door to grab some food. She returned with a glass of milk and two cookies that the student gratefully enjoyed.

Twenty-five years later the student had become a senior surgeon in an American hospital. While working there he came across a woman's medical record that stated that her cancer was advanced and that every other hospital had given up on her. He knew that treatment for her would be expensive and difficult, with the chance of her surviving very low. However, he took the case, gathered top specialists, and spent a lot of time helping to treat the patient. Many of the other doctors were confused and surprised with why he was doing so. Yet, his efforts paid off as the woman survived the surgery and the doctors said that she would be able to live for many more years to come. The woman was very happy.

A couple of days later the bill from the hospital arrived in the mail. The woman knew that the treatment was expensive and was expecting a large bill. Nevertheless, when she opened the bill, she instead saw that her bill had been paid and her doctor had instead written: paid twenty-five years ago with a glass of milk and two cookies.

What had happened was that the doctor had recognized the woman's name from her file. He realized that this was the same woman who had given him a glass of milk and two cookies when he was really hungry and in need of food. He had never forgotten that act of kindness and had decided to pay back her kindness and help cure her. Ultimately, that kind and selfless act of giving that woman had conducted twenty-five years ago without expecting anything in return, saved her life. Such is the power of kindful giving.

Every act of kindful giving has the power to change somebody's day. Who knows, maybe it will be the difference between life and death for somebody. Furthermore, with each of these acts of giving, we become closer with the people around us. Our interdependency with each other prospers with this kindful giving and creates happiness in everyone.

Use Gentle Words

Just as your kindful actions have a significant impact on your relationships, so do your words. If you use harsh words when speaking, people will not want to be around you. You will also attract people who value negative thinking and actions and may end up being surrounded by bad influences. Your sense of inter-dependence will wither away as you dwell in a cycle of anger, hatred, or resentment. We all sometimes get stuck in vicious cycles of abusive words, resulting in some lost relationships and then loneliness. Your loneliness may cause you to get bitter and speak more unpleasant words, which will cause more people to distance themselves from you. This cycle will repeat until your language evolves into a more kindful and harmless one.

This practice begins by having a kindful understanding that your own suffering may be caused by your own words. With this understanding, you can become more mindful to prevent yourself from using hurtful words. For instance, if you feel the urge to lie, then remember when a lie has hurt you or someone you know. This can help prevent you from doing so again, but you also need to reflect on why you want to lie. Usually, people lie when they have done something wrong, want to avoid pun-ishment, or because they are concerned with what others might think about them.

Learn to use gentle words by complimenting someone. Even a small compliment can make someone's day better. When you begin complimenting people and notice how it puts a smile on your face, you will do it more often. You will enjoy saying gentle words and will eventually reduce the number of unpleas-ant words you use. You will understand the impact of your words on the people around you. So, the next time you see your neighbour, smile and compliment them.

However, sometimes you may feel upset, angry, sad, or disappointed. Emotions can influence the language you use if you don't remind yourself to be kind when speaking. No matter how upsetting a situation is, you must speak kindfully. Learning to recognize when you are about to say something unpleasant should prevent you from doing so. Instead of cursing when you stub your toe, for example, try using a funny word like "strawberries" or "fudge." Even in a slightly angry tone, it will not harm anyone. If you express your pain through profanities, your pain and anger increases, causing you to carry anger and spread your unhappiness to people around you throughout your day. By using gentle and kindful words, even in the most upsetting situations, you spread happiness to people.

Take Meaningful Action

Just as gentle words can spread happiness, so can meaningful actions. Not only should you take meaningful action toward others, but also take meaningful action toward yourself. Choose to be kindful to yourself as well as to others. Without the intention to also be kind to yourself, you might experience the exhaustion that comes from giving to others without also caring for yourself. You cannot succeed by only giving and caring for others. Similar to how a bird needs both wings to fly, you must take care of and be kindful to yourself as well. You need to learn to balance and conduct both simultaneously. That is why it is as important to do kind actions for others as it is to do kind actions for yourself.

This story by Ajahn Brahm demonstrates how meaningful action can change somebody's life.

What We Really Want

One morning, an abbot woke up to the sound of something moving in the shrine room. He found this unusual as he knew that most of the other monks were sleeping at this time. So, he went to investigate. While investigating he came across the silhouette of a hooded figure standing in the darkness. Unfazed, the abbot kindly asked what the person wanted. The figure harshly demanded the key to the donation box pointing a long, sharp knife at the abbot. Yet, the abbot experienced no fear after seeing the weapon. Instead, he felt compassion for the young man. The abbot agreed and calmly gave the key to the man. The man hurriedly snatched the key and began emptying the donation box. As he was doing this, the abbot noticed how worn-out, tired, and hungry the man appeared. "When was the last time you have eaten, dear boy," the abbot asked, concerned for the man. The man instead barked "shuddup!" to the monk. However, the abbot instead gave directions to the food and invited the man to help himself to the food. This caused the man to pause for a second; he was confused as he was not used to someone being kind to him when he was taking their money. He could not understand the abbot's concern for his welfare. So, he frantically filled his pockets with cash from the donation box and food from the cabinets. Yet, he still held the knife towards the abbot just in case. Finally, he threatened the abbot, shouting, "And don't call the cops, or else!" To this the abbot calmly replied, "Why should I call the police? Those donations are to help poor people like you, and I have freely given you the food. You have stolen nothing. Go in peace." With that the confused burglar left with the cash and food.

The next morning the abbot explained his encounter to his fellow monks and lay committee who were very proud of him. However, a few days' later, the abbot read some news that said that the same burglar had robbed another house. This time he had been caught and sentenced to ten years in jail.

Just over ten years later, the abbot woke up early in the morning to the familiar sound of somebody moving in the shrine room. He went to investigate as he had done ten years earlier and he saw exactly who he had seen ten years earlier. The same dark silhouette stood beside the donation box carrying the same sharp knife. "Remember me?" the man shouted at the abbot. "Yes," replied the abbot as he reached for the key to the donation box in his pocket. Then the man smiled, lowered the knife, and began explaining. He explained how he had remembered the abbot and his kindness when he was in prison. He said that the abbot was the only person who was kind to him and actually cared for his well being. "I realized that last time I took the wrong thing. This time I have come to take your secret of kindness and inner peace," he said. Then, he asked the abbot if he would take him as one of his disciples. Finally, the man became a monk who was full of kindness and inner peace.

This story shows how a practice of kindfulness and meaningful actions was able to change the man's life. The abbot's kindful actions were so meaningful to the man that he remembered him for ten years while he was in prison. Simply showing the man that the abbot cared for his well-being was enough to change the man and help him find the way to happiness and inner peace. Similarly, we must become these beacons of light and hope for people around us. Let us be like lighthouses guiding boats to shore on a dark night. We must help each other become better and must conduct meaningful actions. Especially when people may be struggling and experiencing difficult situations. By doing so, we will be able to give a helping hand to the people who need it. Our meaningful actions can help people evolve into more kindful and happier versions of themselves. As we are doing these meaningful actions, we will also be helping our-selves grow into more kindful people.

Develop a Sense of Equity

While you conduct meaningful acts of giving and speak gentle words, you should also develop a sense of equity. Consider the following quote:

> The term "equity" refers to fairness and justice and is distinguished from equality: Whereas equality means providing the same to all, equity means recognizing that we do not all start from the same place and must acknowledge and make adjustments to imbalances. The process is ongoing, requiring us to identify and overcome intentional and unintentional barriers arising from bias or systemic structures.
>
> — NACE CENTER

Without equity, you will not be able to develop a complete understanding of interdependency. Just as you do not want others to harm you, others do not want you to harm them. Just as you would like to live a happy life, others also want to live a happy life. As you develop this understanding, along with meaningful actions and gentle speech, you will be able to treat yourself and others with respect and dignity, creating happiness among each other.

Adopting this principle of equity also means recognizing that there is not always a level playing field. There are people who are disadvantaged or face significant hurdles, such as accessing the same rights, medical treatment, housing, or job opportuni-ties because of systemic discrimination and injustice. Women, immigrants, refugees, LGBTQ+ and non-binary people, visible minorities, Indigenous peoples, neuro-divergent peoples, and those who possess an intersection of multiple of these factors, have all been historically and are currently prejudiced by systems that function to prioritize the dominant class. You should particularly attune yourself to how you can actively help and invest energy, time, and resources. You should ask yourself the critical question "What are you willing to give up to ensure equity is embodied in all aspects of a kindful society?"

With this practice of interdependency, you will be able to understand that everyone's safety, prosperity, success, and well-being are based on this interconnectedness. It is key to creating the ideal kindful world. By tuning yourself to others and the world around you, and treating others with the four principles, you can all live in peace and harmony.

CHAPTER 16

Mindfulness for Mental Health and Wellness

"Contemplatives, the four kinds of mindfulness meditation are the path to convergence. They exist to purify beings, overcome sorrow, make an end of pain and suffering, and to realize freedom."

— GAUTAMA BUDDHA

Mental health and wellness are key components to the sustainability of world peace and harmony. Every citizen of every nation would benefit from mindfulness meditation training from a young age. This would help young citizens grow up with wellness at the forefront of their lifestyle and intentions. Similar to going to the gym for physical fitness, mindfulness meditation training centres for mental and emotional fitness could be built in every city. We need to think seriously about radical changes like this to address the stress, anxiety, depression, sadness, fear, and guilt that many of us experience.

Mindfulness Meditation in Action

As a mindfulness meditation practitioner and teacher, I encourage my students to practise mindfulness meditation as a form of self-care and mental health remedy. Mindfulness meditation is not a religious practice. Rather, it is a universal practice that anyone can benefit from. It is a self-transformation intentional practice that helps your mind go from being unmindful to mindful, unfocused to focused, negative to positive, unhealthy to healthy, unkind to kind, harmful to harmless, unhappy to happy, and unsteady to still.

So why should you consider practising mindfulness meditation? One reason lies within modern psychology and neuroscience research, which show the many benefits of meditation. On a personal note, for the past twenty-seven years, I have conducted weekly mindfulness meditation sessions for the public, and for twenty-two years, I have offered one-day mindfulness meditation retreats to the public in Canada. I have offered similar sessions throughout North America, Europe, and Asia. Attendees were of different faiths, traditions, and social and cultural backgrounds. People of all ages attended these sessions and retreats voluntarily.

I know that people are seeking a way to inner peace and happiness. They are going through emotional struggles and are seeking solutions. Doctors, psychologists, psychotherapists, and counsellors are beginning to talk more and more about mindfulness meditation as a wellness therapy for the daily stress and anxieties people are experiencing. Though this meditation trend is growing, medication was—and, in some cases, still is—the go-to for all forms of emotional problems and wounds. It was often prescribed without considering alternatives or supportive therapies. When the public comes to meditate with us, I don't ask why they come, who they are, or what their background is.

When I see that they continue to attend sessions every week, and even begin to bring their friends and colleagues, I know that it is helping them heal. I also do individual spiritual counselling, while encouraging the practice of meditation as therapy and healing.

During my meditation training, my meditation teacher told me the following story. It demonstrates the importance of mindfulness meditation.

The Boatman and the Professor

One day a professor went on a journey to a friend's village. On the way to the village, the professor had to cross a big river, yet, there was no bridge. She saw that there was a boatman who was waiting for a passenger to come and cross the river. The professor got up on the boat and sat down. The boatman greeted the professor with a big smile and much respect, and slowly started paddling the boat. The professor who was well learned and possessed a lot of knowledge about various subject matters got into a conversation with the boatman.

The professor asked the boatman, "Do you know about science?"
The boatman said, "No, ma'am."
The professor asked the boatman, "Do you know biology?"
The boatman said, "No, ma'am."
The professor asked the boatman, "Do you know chemistry?"
The boatman said, "No, ma'am."
The professor asked the boatman, "Do you know medical science?"
The boatman said, "No, ma'am."
The professor asked the boatman, "Do you know health science?"
The boatman said, "No, ma'am."
The professor asked the boatman, "Do you know mathematics?"

The boatman said, "No, ma'am."

The professor asked the boatman, "Do you know philosophy?"

The boatman said, "No, ma'am."

The professor asked the boatman, "Do you know sociology and anthropology?"

The boatman said, "No, ma'am."

The professor asked the boatman, "Do you know about the arts?"

The boatman said, "No, ma'am."

The professor asked the boatman, "Do you know about political science?"

The boatman said, "No, ma'am."

To all the professor's questions, the boatman simply replied, "No."

The professor was surprised to meet a man who did not learn the basic sciences, and she said this to the boatman, "Oh boatman, it seems you have wasted your life. You haven't learned any kind of science. How can you make a living?"

As the boatman kept paddling his boat slowly, his boat came to the middle of the river. The boatman was an innocent man and he asked the professor whether he could ask a question or not. The professor granted him the opportunity to ask the question.

Boatman: "Professor, this conversation made me realize that you know all kinds of sciences. Have you studied swimology?"

Professor: "I have studied most of the sciences, but it seems I haven't studied swimology. What is this swimology?"

Boatman: "Well, swimology is an art about how to swim in the water. You need to learn about swimming and saving your life if you fall into the water. Professor, there is a hurricane coming and it will turn over my boat. This is beyond my control. If you don't know how to swim, you may sink and die."

Just as the boatman predicted, the winds quickly picked up, the waves became choppy, and eventually the professor and the boatman were in the midst of a full-blown hurricane, their creaky vessel being flung about. The boatman, who knew only swimology, was able to swim and save his life. The professor who knew all sciences except swimology was not able to swim and she got swept away by the water. The professor was not able to save her life.

Swimology and Kindfulness

Swimology is kindfulness. This is a new science that should be taught to all students from junior and senior kindergarten to college and university. These students are the future generation. These students are future policymakers, politicians, teachers, professors, scientists, philosophers, psychologists, etc. Because of extreme greed, anger, ignorance, jealousy, pride, and ego, human beings often create the tornadoes, typhoons, and hurricanes of violence, war, bigotry, racism, sexism, and hatred. No matter how much knowledge we have about our modern education, if we are lacking knowledge of kindfulness, we may not be able to save ourselves from the hurricanes of life. Kindfulness science should be offered at every education institution in every country of the world and should be taught for every global citizen's well-being. Kindfulness policy should be introduced to the United Nations for the sustainable peace and happiness of the world. For this, I have a song that most people may recognize. It goes like this:

> Row, row, row, your boat
> Gently down the stream
> Merrily, merrily, merrily, merrily
> Life is but a dream.

Row, row, row, your life
Gently down the road
Mindfully kindfully mindfully kindfully
Life is but a dream.

The moral to the song is: Kindfulness is the bridge.

Cultivating Mindfulness

Living mindfully means living safely in every moment. Living mindfully means holding a flashlight that helps us see the path clearly so that we can avoid walking into a puddle of mud.

The practice of mindfulness is like having a security guard. The task of the security guard is to protect people inside and check everyone who is entering and exiting. The security guard would prevent any visitor who endangers the safety of their charges from entering the venue. In the same way, mindfulness practices help us guard our own mind. Incoming or visiting negative thoughts can destroy peace of mind.

The security guard is the meditation practitioner whose task it is to remain vigilant. It is similar to how a country remains vigilant by having the most powerful anti-missile shields possible in order to protect the nation from potential enemy missiles. Mindfulness practices function like a border security guard who screens handbags and luggage. If they find prohibited items, they remove them. The story that follows teaches an important lesson on danger.

The Hunter and the Monkey

In the Himalayas, there is an area that humans and animals, like monkeys and deer, inhabit. In this area, there was once a hunter who wanted to catch a monkey for a local delicacy—monkey stew! The hunter created a trap, using chemical poisons and metal framed bars to catch a monkey. The hunter set up the device by some nearby trees where he deduced a family of monkeys resided. After setting up the device, the hunter went into hiding. All the monkeys on the trees saw the device which was shining beautifully as the sun rays ricocheted off the polished metal bars. It looked suspicious to all of the monkeys except one. This monkey was curious and he was slowly descending the tree to inquire about the device. All the other monkeys tried to convince him not to go there and touch it, squealing horrendously at him, but he ignored them. This monkey was stubborn.

This monkey went to the device. The top of the device shimmered with the rays of the morning sun, and the monkey could not resist his urge to touch it with his right hand. Alas, the monkey's right hand got trapped in the metal bars, and stuck to the poison. The monkey was terrified, and he tried to free his right hand by using the support of his left hand. Yet, when the monkey placed his left hand onto the device, it got stuck as well. Now the monkey started panicking. He began thinking of how he could free himself as he knew that nobody was coming to rescue him. The monkey decided to use his right foot to free his hands by placing his right foot on the device and pushing away. Yet, this only caused his right foot to get stuck. Now the monkey's heartbeat was skyrocketing. He was screaming for help. Yet, no other monkeys dared to go there and fall into the trap. They all watched what was unfolding for the stubborn monkey. The monkey thought that he would use his left foot to free the two hands and the right foot. No doubt you know what happened next. All of his limbs were stuck. The monkey started crying desperately for help, but nobody came to help. The monkey decided that the only chance for him to free his two hands and feet from the device was to use his mouth. So, the monkey placed his mouth on the device, getting his mouth glued as well. Thus, the monkey was now helpless.

Meanwhile, the hunter was watching everything unfold and he saw that the monkey remained completely stuck and helpless. Seeing this, the hunter came and picked up the monkey with the device and went home to enjoy his meal.

We can learn several things from this story. The first of which is that there are territories we should prevent ourselves from going to. They are dangerous and detrimental to us. Some examples are as follows:

The territory of violence
The territory of war
The territory of inequality
The territory of racial discrimination
The territory of injustice
The territory of unkindness
The territory of hatred and anger
The territory of intolerance
The territory of greed
The territory of selfishness
The territory of disrespect
The territory of not receiving education

These territories are detrimental and dangerous. They cause deaths. We should be mindful of that. What are the territories suitable for us to live our lives in harmony, side by side?

The territory of nonviolence
The territory of peace

The territory of equality
The territory of acceptance, non-discrimination
The territory of justice
The territory of kindness
The territory of love
The territory of forgiveness
The territory of tolerance
The territory of generosity
The territory of selflessness
The territory of respect
The territory of education

While we are being mindful to prevent and eliminate unsafe and unhealthy territories, we have to be mindful to allow ourselves to be in safe and healthy territories by cultivating and sustaining safe and healthy territories. This is for our own well-being. As we are building this ideal world for ourselves, we also have to help people around us and beyond do the same for everyone's well-being.

The unsafe and unhealthy territories are the creations or products of our own defiled minds, and the safe and healthy territories are the creations and products of our own purified mind. Our mind is a powerful tool. The misguided and unguarded mind creates unhealthy territories, and a guided and guarded mind creates healthy territories. We have to learn and practise mindfulness meditation to guide, guard, develop, and free our own mind. All these territories are projections and reflections of our own mind and are rooted in internal tendencies and emotions. External factors can trigger our internal tendencies. If we have no control of this, we will fall into trouble. How can we control and calm ourselves? Let me tell you another story that will shed light.

The Fox and the Turtle

A turtle one day was seeking food by the bank of a river. At the same time a fox also came out from its den to seek food. The fox saw the turtle and he was relieved to see some good food walking by the bank of the river. He was thrilled and aimed at the turtle to catch it. The fox was stealthily moving toward the turtle. The turtle saw the fox coming toward it. The turtle was thinking of running away but he realized that he was not fast enough. Running away was not going to work. Calmly the turtle thought of a way of saving his life. Suddenly the turtle had an eureka moment. The turtle realized that if he chose to recede into his hard shell, the fox would be unable to do anything. With this eureka moment the turtle was relieved. So when the fox came close and pounced to grab the turtle, the turtle went inside its hard shell. Thus, the fox could not grab the turtle.

The fox was hovering around the turtle with the intention of grabbing the turtle as soon as it stuck any of its limbs out. Yet, the turtle was safe inside and realized that he would be safe as long as he remained inside the shell. The turtle was thinking, "Of course, I am tired and hungry. My enemy is still hovering around me wanting to grab and kill me, but I am safe here. My shell is hard and it is my protection. My enemy, the fox cannot grab and harm me. Despite my tiredness and hunger, let me stay inside patiently and calmly."

As the turtle remained inside, the fox got tired of hovering around. It abandoned the mission and went away. The turtle sensed that his enemy the fox was no longer hovering around and it slowly came back out and continued searching for food again.

By and large I tell this story to make people realize the significance of mindfulness meditation practice. First, we have to be mindful of the enemies that come in the guise of a fox. Who are our foxes? We can encounter our foxes at work, at home, in the neighbourhood, or anywhere we go. "Our foxes" could be difficult people at work and at home or challenging and difficult situations. These are physical foxes. There are many emotional and psychological foxes as well, such as stress, tension, anxiety, panic attacks, depression, worry, fear, sadness, pain, and guilt. The foxes could be past thinking, future thinking, negative stories, or holding onto negative mental images. The foxes are the hurricanes, tornadoes, and typhoons in life, tornadoes of anger, violence, and unrest.

Look at this story and what strategy the turtle followed when he encountered an enemy, the fox. We should remember that mindfulness is strong and that it can protect us. Withdraw, go inward, and remain in your own zone. The present moment is our green zone, the safe zone.

When you stay in the present moment with calmness, still-ness and much patience, the enemy cannot get you. The enemy cannot harm you. The enemy cannot do anything. In fact, the enemy is going to get frustrated and disappointed. At the end, the enemy leaves you. Mindfulness meditation is a technique that empowers you with calmness, stillness, clarity, and insight, all of which are essential requirements to overcoming any tough circumstance in life.

CHAPTER 17

Mindfulness Meditation Technique: SSMK

"If you have time to breathe you have time to meditate."

— Ajahn Amaro

Now that you know the benefits of remaining calm and mindful, how do you do it? How do you make your mind still? Try SSMK, a simple mindfulness breathing meditation technique. SSMK stands for: Slowly, Silently, Mindfully, Kindfully.

There is an art to breathing. Breath is life. Everyone breathes. Follow these steps to learn this art of breathing.

1. Find a quiet place and assume a comfortable and relaxed posture.
2. Become a turtle by withdrawing and going inside your own shell. This is your green and safe zone.
3. Slowly and gently close your eyes. Take a deep breath and let your entire body go into relaxation.
4. Now bring your full attention to the air that is entering and leaving through your nostrils. Breathe in and breathe out slowly. Breathing in and out slowly will help your body become stable.

5. As you keep breathing slowly, see if you can do this in complete silence, breathing in silently and out silently. Breathing in and out slowly and breathing in and out silently will help your mind become very still.

6. To help your body become stable and your mind become still, keep breathing in and out with 100 percent attention. Be mindful and keep your full attention on your breath only. Follow your breath all the way in and all the way out.

7. During this process of making your body stable and your mind still, be mindful to add a lot of kindness. Be gentle, soft, and kind to your body and mind. Breathe in and out kindfully. This is really caring for yourself. Allow yourself to be full of kindness. Kindness has the power to heal you in the moment. This will help you sustain your still and tranquil mind, and this is the fountain of bliss, joy, inner happiness, and inner peace.

Part Four
The Hope For a Kindful World

CHAPTER 18

The Four Powers of Effort

"Hope is being able to see that there is light despite all of the darkness."

—DESMOND TUTU

Hope and faith can be sustained with four powers of effort. Our goal, first, is to make ourselves mindful and kind, and secondly, make others mindful and kind. We have faith in ourselves, and we can hope for a mindful and kind nation. To accomplish this, effort is a fundamental requirement we all need to have and cultivate in order to keep up the flame of a mindful and kind nation. Let us be mindful that the effort must be nurtured with the following four powers that are the fuel of effort. Without fuel or gas, a car cannot be driven to go to its destination. Our destination is to make ourselves and others mindful and kind.

Power of Rejection

For everyone's well-being, all unkind and negative tendencies in our behaviour, habit, attitude, and mentality must be rejected. Violence, war, inequality, racial discrimination, injustice, unkindness, hatred and anger, intolerance, greed and stinginess, selfishness and self-centredness, disrespect, bigotry, and phobias must be rejected. Why reject? Because these tendencies are the root causes of social disharmony and war. An effort must be made to reject these negative tendencies, which can be seen in our society and the world.

First, I have to ask myself if I have such negative tendencies. What benefits do I have in holding onto them? Are these harmful to me, harmful to others, and harmful to all? If, through mindful reflection, we realize that the answer is, "Yes, I have these negative and unkind tendencies and they are causing me problems and they are causing problems to others," we should be mindful to make an effort to reject them, abandon them, and let them go. By eliminating such negative tendencies, we can find peace within, and our peace will not be a threat to anyone, anywhere we go.

Power of Aspiration

In accomplishing a goal, aspiration helps us to initiate a mission. Our mission has to be clear. Aspiration comes from realizing that we can bring a positive change in the world and help the world become a better place to live in peace and harmony.

The power of aspiration has the capability of eliminating all kinds of weaknesses and faults we human beings have. We eliminate our own weaknesses, and we help others eliminate their weaknesses. Eradicating a weakness may take a long time, but we should never give up. Light cannot be seen overnight. It may take many days and nights to eradicate the darkness of unkindness and bring light to kindness. We go slowly, with great ambition, and acquire good qualities for ourselves and others. Good qualities have to be cultivated today with the hope that we can be mindful and kind just as others can be mindful and kind. Our effort is to train ourselves at least with one good quality or one act of kindness a day.

Nobel Peace laureate Nelson Mandela's life is a typical example. He realized his own faults and weaknesses. He also realized that he has some hidden strengths and powers of forgiveness, tolerance, equality, justice, and peace. When he got released from prison, he left with a new vision and aspiration. He voluntarily and intentionally gave up the intention of taking revenge. He mindfully undertook a good quality of forgiveness to transform himself, the nation, and the world. He became a champion of this light, which made him a global icon of peace and freedom. He became a much talked about and highly respected figure in the global stage. This is the power of aspiration.

Power of Steadfastness

In navigating ourselves toward a mindful and kind nation, we will certainly encounter adversities like doubt, fear, rejection, pessimism, ego conflicts, and haters. There could be all kinds of obstacles. On the road to our goal and dream, if we encounter hurdles, we have to overcome them with steadfastness. Without steadfastness, patience, and forbearance, nothing can be won.

Power of Joy

When an effort is made to reject negative tendencies, when an effort is made to cultivate aspiration, and when this is done with steadfastness, joy will arise. A mind full of joy will never trigger violent acts. A happy and joyful mind is a real blessing. Joyful minds can heal all emotional wounds. We have to make ourselves happy and healthy. A happy and healthy mind is a happy, healthy nation!

CHAPTER 19

Final words

"May you be well; may you be happy and peaceful."

Without loving-kindness for humanity, our collective existence will be at risk and danger. It is the faith and hope for a harmonious and peaceful world that we are coming together for, so that we all can live side by side in peace and harmony. As you read this book, you may have an obvious question: Is this peaceful world and idea of making a mindful and kind nation a mere dream, or is that a reality? In a famous speech, Dr. Martin Luther King, Jr. told a large audience in Washington, DC, "I have a dream." Indeed, we all need to have a dream. This dream is my vision for the world—that is to see a nation that peaceful, mindful, and kind, for the betterment of humanity, and eventually, to see a whole world of kindfulness. I have deep love and appreciation for humanity. All of the kindful activities I have been doing over the past three decades have been done not for glory, praise, or fame, but solely for the love and kindness of my own humanity and the humanity of all those around me. I have been driven by this dream for a long time. I have embarked on the journey to build a mindful and kind nation for a long time, and I have spoken about it at various occasions in my role as a public figure. People of all ages and backgrounds have expressed appreciation and gratitude for this vision, which has in turn given me more courage and strength to keep going with this vision.

To make this dream real, we have to connect with like-minded people around the world, people who really care for each other. We have not yet lost humanity. There are amazing people who are truly kind to one another and who are extending their kind and generous help to alleviate human suffering.

Faith in kindfulness and hope for a world that honours the best in our humanity is what gives us courage to go toward harmony in the face of adversity and honour the unity of diversity. How do we sustain this faith and hope so that the dream does not simply die? Let me tell you a short story that my grandfather told me when I was a child. It is about a squirrel family.

The Faith and Hope of Squirrel Parents

Once upon a time, there lived a squirrel family on a tree located by the beach. One day, a monstrous wave hit the tree and carried away the baby squirrel. The squirrel parents were saddened, yet they were determined to move all the water of the ocean to find and save the life of their baby squirrel. Thus, they began pondering over a mechanism to move the water. All they could figure out was to move the water with their tail. With the intention of rescuing the baby squirrel, the squirrel parents started moving water with their tails.

We understand the size of the ocean and the volume of the water it contains. One may question the effort the squirrel parents were making. Nevertheless, the squirrel parents kicked into high gear, furiously paddling with their tails. They had faith in their action and hoped to rescue the baby squirrel because they had deep love for their baby squirrel. The baby squirrel was their life—the next generation. They had faith in their ability and the means of saving the baby squirrel. They were determined. Doing something is much better than doing nothing! So, they paddled and paddled until they finally saw their baby squirrel struggling in the water. They had saved him.

Our beautiful humanity is also threatened by a giant wave of violence, unkindness, phobia, racial discrimination, war, and global unrest. We can move all such negative elements by coming together. We are no squirrels. In fact, we are humans. We are not just humans; rather, we are very intelligent human beings. There are some elements of the world that are creating these waves, and if we allow them to come everyday, these waves are going to destroy our humanity. We can minimize and alleviate these monster waves with kindness and mindfulness.

All global citizens may not be able to be aligned with everything, but we can be aligned, at least, with bona fide kindness and mindfulness. I strongly believe we all are aligned with kindness and mindfulness. This is the channel and bridge of kindfulness through which we connect with all global citizens.

We may not know if we will succeed like the squirrel parents did, but we will at least know what it looks like to try in spite of hate, bigotry, racism, sexism, violence, war, and pandemics. Let us try to honour what it means to be human—our unending, relentless ability to find hope, in even the darkest of places, and channel that hope into positive action.

A thousand candles can be lit from one candle. If one citizen of a country chooses to become the light of kindness and mindfulness, this one citizen can influence another thousand citizens to become mindful and kind.

Through this work, our effort is to bring the hope of a glimpse of light to the people who are living in darkness of violence, war, and the negativities of the world. The following story helps illustrate this.

Cave Men and the Light

Once there lived a man in a cave and he got used to the dark surroundings of the cave. He lived in that complete darkness for such a long time that he thought it was his whole world. He would stumble here and there and get hurt by falling. It was his misery, but he never realized he was suffering from stumbling and getting hurt, as he knew nothing else. One day the cave man saw a strange and tiny glimpse of light. He was curious to know what it was. His curiosity led him to go toward the glimpse of light. As he kept moving towards it, the glimpse of light turned brighter and brighter. This made the caveman more inquisitive to explore what it was. Eventually the tiny glimpse of light made the caveman go out of the cave where he finally saw the sun, the blue sky and the beautiful trees for the first time. The cave man never went back to the darkness in the cave!

Similarly imagine a sailor in a boat, lost in the ocean during the night looking for the shore. If the sailor sees a beam of light, she will head toward it to save herself from drowning in the water.

In ancient times, ships trying to cross the ocean used a bird that flew in the sky. In those days, they did not have radar. The captain of the ship looking for a shore would release the bird. The bird flew away, and if it could not see a shore, it would return to the ship. If the bird kept flying without returning to the ship, however, the captain knew there was a shore and would pilot the ship toward that direction. Our hope of kindfulness is like this bird.

Before concluding this book, I would like to tell you another story. I remember my grandfather telling us this story as we kids sat on the ground in front of him. My grandfather took a deep breath and told the story.

The Hummingbird and the Vulture

Children, among many birds, there are two types of birds living side by side on a mountain. They are the vultures and humming-birds. Vultures don't look beautiful, but hummingbirds, on the other hand, are enticingly elegant. A cemetery is located near this mountain. The vultures fly in the sky looking for dead animals or human corpses that are thrown into the cemetery. Dead bodies are food for vultures. If the vultures see the dead bodies in the cemetery ground, they land and consume them. They always fly in the sky of the cemetery to find a dead body. In the same cemetery, there are flowers and berry bushes. The hummingbirds fly in the same sky with an intention of finding a flower full of nectar. If the humming-birds see the flower bushes, they land and hum around the flower. They sip the nectar from the flower without destroying it. Nectar is the delightful food of the hummingbirds. My dear children, now you have a choice, whether to become a vulture or a hummingbird. If you choose to become a vulture, you are going to seek out that which is unpleasant. You will appear ravenous and hungry like vultures. If you choose to become a hummingbird, you are going to search and eat nectar, and you are going to delight in the beautiful joys of life.

When my grandfather told the story, we all replied, "Grandfather, we want to become the hummingbirds. We don't want to become vultures." My grandfather was very happy to hear that we kids wanted to become hummingbirds!

Who is this vulture in our world? Who is this hummingbird? We can see vulture-like people living in the world. We also see the hummingbird-like people. Unkindness repels us. Kindness is beautiful and draws us near to one another. Unkindness is like already being a dead body. Kindness is like living in a field of nectar. Dead bodies invite the vultures, and flowers full of nectar invite the hummingbirds!

Be mindful of this difference. Be mindful not to become a vulture. Be mindful to become a hummingbird. Our hope is to find the flower; our hope is to become a flower full of nectar. Our hope is to plant the seed of a beautiful flower that will become full of nectar and attract other hummingbirds. Our hope is to transform ourselves into hummingbirds.

Manifesting our True Potential Through the Mind

We human beings are equipped with a powerful tool. That is our mind. Generally, people tend to believe in manifestations—such as manifesting the winning lottery numbers or manifesting our dream career—yet they don't know where such manifestations can be manifested through. It is our powerful mind that manifests what we want in life. The most powerful mind can be directed to manifest both bad and good, unkindness and kindness, negativity and positivity, darkness and light.

We are training our minds to not manifest the bad, unkindness, negativity, and darkness. We are training our minds to manifest all good, kindness, positivity, and light. I have been dreaming, thinking, visualizing, imagining, and manifesting a kind and mindful individual, nation, and world for a long time. Those who know me and have attended my public talks and meditation sessions know about this matter. I have encouraged the public to manifest such a nation and world, and the public has in turn encouraged me to continue manifesting joy for them through my teachings and meditations. If all citizens choose to manifest such a world, a mindful and kind nation can be materialized in the not-too-distant future.

The modern generation is getting tired of the old fashion of war, violence, and manipulation. Our new generation wants peace, harmony, mental well-being, and kindness. Unkindness is an old style. Kindness is the new fashion.

While the majority of the world's population is racing around in the darkness, our effort is to help the world slow down and move intentionally. We do this with a heart full of kindness for the well-being and peace of all of humanity. Running around in the darkness will hurt not only oneself, but also everyone else. Unkindness will destroy humanity's coexistence. As a conscious and kindful global community, let us not be dejected. Let us be determined to plant the seeds of mindfulness and kindness with a hope and dream of a kindful world. I believe a kindful world can be seen in the near future with a culture of mindfulness and kindness if we all choose to become mindful and kind. Let us be kindful to ourselves. Let us be kindful to others. Let us become the light from which many thousands of candles can be lit. Just as the one monkey inspired the hundred monkeys to wash and eat the mangoes, let us inspire one another with kindfulness.

Let us look at each other with kindful eyes. Let us hear and listen with kindful ears. Let us smell with kindfulness. Let us taste with kindfulness. Let us touch with kindfulness. Let us do kindful deeds. Let us speak kindful words. Let us think kindful thoughts. This is our hope for a peaceful world, with a culture of mindfulness and kindness.

Acknowledgements

My Students and Friends:

Ginette Young, Tristan Mohamed, Samindra Priyarathna, Amber Nancarrow, Ryan Joseph, Sheila McCallum, Mitch Abrams, Michael & Carol Weldon, Troy MacLean, Dinushi Fernando, Nimal Priyarathna, Jenny Kim, John Tan, Jenny Miotke, Anthony Veres, Diane Lauzon, Dave & Rani Dhaliwal, Tiffanie Caracassis, Peter Tolias, Michael Nguyen, Aloy Perera, David & Minnie Lai, Darshan Chaudhary, Shireen Ooi

My Teachers:

The Late Most Venerable Madihe Pannasiha Maha Nayaka Mahathera

The Late Most Venerable Ampitiye Sri Rahula Nayaka Mahathera

The Most Venerable Gyanasree Mahathera, the 13th Sangharaja

The Most Venerable Brahmanagama Muditha Nayaka Mahathera

The Most Venerable Kulugammana Dhammawasa Nayaka Mahathera

My Parents:

The Late Mr. Pulin Bihari Barua

The Late Mrs. Dipthi Rani Barua

Notes

Chapter 1. Vision for a Kindful Nation

Canadian Index of Wellbeing, *The 2016 CIW National Report*, *https://uwaterloo.ca/canadian-index-wellbeing/*, Faculty of Applied Health Sciences, University of Waterloo, 2016.

Woodcock, George, *The Canadians*, Harvard University Press, 1980.

World Happiness Report 2023, worldhappiness.report/ed/2023.

Mackenzie, Lewis, *Peacekeeper: The Road to Sarajevo*, Douglas & McIntyre Ltd., 1993.

One Hundred Monkeys: A story the author heard from the owner of The Hundredth Monkey Bookstore in Toronto.

Chapter 2. Understanding the Journey

The Quest for Happiness: Wheelwright, Joseph B. *The Reality of the Psyche*. New York: Putnam, 1968.

Chapter 3. The Art of Kindness

The Pair of Acrobats: Bodhi, Bhikkhu, *A New Translation of the Samyutta Nikaya, Volume I*, Wisdom Publications, 2000.

Chapter 5. Caring for Others: Four Ways

Harris, Thomas Anthony *I'm Ok-You're Ok*, Galahad, 2004

Brown, Brené, https://brenebrown.com.

Chapter 10: Climate Change

The Parrot Twins: Cowell, E. B. *The Jātaka, Volume 3*, based on the Sattigumba Jātaka (No. 503), Pali Text Society, 1990.

Chapter 13. The Kindful Tree

Goleman, Daniel, *Working with Emotional Intelligence*, Bantam, 2000.

The Kindful Kingdom: Bodhi, Bhikkhu, a Translation of the Anguttara Nikaya, Wisdom Publication, Boston, 2012.

The Sage, the Pig Farmer, and his Nightmares: A story told by the Venerable Buddhananda.

The Hawk and the Quail: Sakunagghi Sutta: *The Hawk, based on a translation* by the VenerableThanissaro Bhikkhu, 1997.

Chapter 14. Kindfulness and Interdependency

Ubuntu: an African philosophy/concept shared with His Holiness Dalai Lama by a delegation of South African academics.

Chapter 15. The Practice of Kindful Interdependence

Milk and Cookies, What We Really Want: Brahm, Ajahn, *Who Ordered This Truckload of Dung?: Inspiring Stories for Welcoming Life's Difficulties, Wisdom Publications, 2005.*

Chapter 16. Mindfulness for Mental Health and Wellness

The Boatman and the Professor: a story told at a Vipassana talk by S. N. Goenka, Founder and Teacher of Vipassana Retreat Centres in Asia, Europe and North America.

The Hunter and the Monkey: Bodhi, Bhikkhu, *A New Translation of the Samyutta Nikaya, Volume I,* Wisdom Publications, 2000.

The Fox and the Turtle: Bodhi, Bhikkhu. *A New Translation of the Samyutta Nikaya, Volume I,* Wisdom Publications, 2000)

Chapter 19. Conclusion

The Faith and Hope of Squirrel Parents: Cowell, E. B. *The Jātaka, Volume 3,* based on the Kalandaka Jātaka (No. 548), Pali Text Society, 1990.

Cave Men and the Light: Cooper, John M. and Hutchinson, D. S., *Plato: Complete Works,* based on Plato's The Allegory of the Cave, Hackett Publishing Company, Indianapolis/Cambridge,1997.

The Hummingbird and Vulture: A story told by the author's meditation teacher in Sri Lanka. The same story can be found in *Get Your Hopes Up* by Joyce Meyer.

Printed in Canada

A Welsh Girlhood?

Prologue: Spirit, Are You There?

1. Let's Go Play in the Bomb Buildings + List of the Dead, Teilo Creec + photo or Teilo,
2. The Blue Hats
3. Morgan Le Fay
4. Er Royal Ighness
5. Which One Are You?
6. Don't You Speak Welsh?
7. Miss Hodge.
8. Washing the Graves (Solidify the teacher, new? more.)
9. Is That the Rive- Cydnis?
10. The Sound of the Sea.
11. Last Night When We Were Young.
12. Pwll Du.
13. One Dark Misty Rainy Night.

- Which One Are You?
- Er Royal Igh
  Glennor
- Miss Hodge
- Is that the river? Cydnis.
- Washing the Graves
- Don't You Speak
- Last Night When We Were Young.
- The Sound of the Sea
- One Dark Misty Rainy Night.
  Pwll Du.

Photos -
1. { Bombed houses
     Leene & me superimposed
2. Lorna & me age 10
3. Teilo Concert. (opp list names)
4. Another photo.